# LEGAL A

G000089090

★ Contract and Deed examined.

★ Extra suspensive conditions written.

★ Outline planning permissions arranged and planning matters checked.

★ Off-plan sales taken care of.

★ French inheritance laws explained and solutions proposed.

★ French taxation: its impact on you explained

★ Winding up of French and UK Estates. It's complicated. We do it.

★ French litigation: handled through French Advocates. Pre-determined package fees in most situations.

More information on our website:
**www.seanoconnor.co.uk**

## SEAN O'CONNOR & CO

### Bilingual Solicitors

**2 River Walk, Tonbridge, Kent TN9 1DT
Tel: 01732 365 378  Fax: 01732 360 144**
E-mail: seanoconnorco@aol.com

# French Law

## For Property Buyers

Edited by Kerry Schrader

Published by French Property News

Second edition - published in Great Britain in 2007 by
**French Property News**
**Archant House, Oriel Road, Cheltenham, Glos GL50 1BB**
**www.french-property-news.com**

The information contained in this book is offered for consideration
and should not be acted upon without independent advice from
suitably qualified professionals.

Whilst every effort has been made to ensure the accuracy of this
work, no responsibility for any loss occasioned as a result of acting
on any material therein can be accepted by the Publisher, Editor
or any Contributor to this publication.

**Copyright © 2007 French Property News**

All rights reserved. This publication may not be reproduced, stored in a
retrieval system or transmitted in any form either electrical, mechanical or
otherwise without the written consent of the owner of the copyright.

ISBN 978-0-9515861-2-9

# CONTENTS

# Foreword

This is the second edition of "French law for property buyers." The first edition was published in 1997.

Legal articles have always been one of the most popular and important features in *French Property News* and this is a collection of articles which appeared in that publication as originals between 2003 and 2007.

The articles are written by individuals from two bilingual legal firms. Sean O'Connor of Sean O' Connor and Co is a member of the Institute of Linguists (French) and a member of the Institute of Translation and Interpreting (French). Several senior staff members from Blake Lapthorn Tarlow Lyons have contributed articles, most prominent among them being Philippe Piedon-Lavaux, Notaire and Honorary Consul of France since 2002. The articles cover a wide range of topics relating to buying and owning a property in France.

Readers should take note that the exchange rates, tax rates etc mentioned are those that applied at the date of the article and may have changed. It is not intended that this book should be used as a do-it-yourself legal manual but as a general guide for those considering a property purchase in France.

As the articles contain summary references to some general and specific French laws, the Authors, Editor and Publisher will not accept responsibility or liability for errors or omissions arising from the use of the information contained in the articles. It is recommended, therefore, that readers seek specific, qualified legal advice as it relates to their individual circumstances.

# Ensure you insure

**By Philippe Piedon-Lavaux    January 2003**

Generally speaking British people prefer to purchase a house in France rather than a flat and when undertaking restoration or building work, they quite often ask for a builder in France who is a compatriot. Others have sufficient knowledge to build or restore a house themselves.

However, the construction of a building is a complex operation, and in the same vein as all complicated matters, insurance is needed to cover the risk of a defect in the construction of the building. This is similar to the Buildmark Warranty and Insurance in the UK.

Since 4 January 1978 (French Law 78-12), there has been a very precise law in France regarding builders' insurance. All builders should be aware of the insurance which has to be taken out and the penalties which they will incur if they do not do so.

In the event that insurance has not been taken out, the consequences are serious if the owner wants to sell the property within 10 years from the completion of the building.

**Mandatory insurances**

These two policies are *l'assurance dommage-ouvrage* and *l'assurance responsabilité*. However, more and more insurance companies offer builders a sort of comprehensive policy called *police unique de chantier* for a building site, which brings together the two mandatory policies.

*L'assurance dommage-ouvrage* insures the building and applies to the defects described under article 1792 of the Civil Code – namely all defects which can alter the structure of the building or prevent its normal use. The insurance company is not entitled to ask for an excess payment from the ultimate beneficiaries or property owners.

The insurance company covers this risk for 10 years from completion of the work. On this basis the company undertakes to do repairs without seeking to find who is responsible for the defects. It is sufficient to establish that a defect covered by the policy exists.

The policy benefits not only the present owner of the property but also potential successors for the 10 years from completion of the work.

The owner must be able to prove at any time that he has taken out the mandatory policies by producing evidence. If the owner cannot do so, the sanctions are serious (up to 76,000 euros' fine unless the house has been built for the owner's personal use). However, the builder is normally still responsible if any defects appear and he will have to pay for the damage. In theory, his responsibility cannot be avoided.

By contrast with the *assurance dommage-ouvrage* which covers the building, the *assurance responsabilité* covers the works of the builder for 10 years from the completion of the works he has carried out.

### The notaire's role

Article L243-2 of the insurance code states that in all conveyance deeds for a property less than 10 years old, the notaire has the duty to indicate references to the insurance. In that case, and even in the *compromis* or *promesse de vente*, the notaire has to ask the vendor to bring forward evidence that the construction has been properly insured.

If the vendor has not taken any insurance, then the notaire notifies the purchaser and states in the deed that the purchaser is aware of the situation and the vendor knows that he is responsible for the 10 years from completion of the building. Never be persuaded to waive the right to exercise any recourse against the vendor.

If the notaire forgets to indicate the position regarding the building insurance and if the policies have not been taken out, then the purchaser can ask for the damages from the notaire where the vendor cannot pay for the repairs.

### Before not after

It is an obvious point but it is always important to be properly insured when buying a new property. One must bear in mind that it is easier to get insurance before the works start, but extremely difficult to regularise the situation several months later.

All builders and purchasers of a French property less than 10 years old must take account of the issue of insurance.

# Home improvements

**By Sean O'Connor    February 2003**

It is a lovely spring morning. There you are stepping out of the front door of your French property into your garden. You take a deep breath of fresh air. You feel good. So how is the outside world treating you?

Legally and socially I mean. Let's see. You want to add on a terrace to your property? Go ahead. It won't be included in your permitted surface area for construction purposes. You want to put up a fence around your property? It is automatically permitted under the civil code. Once again, go ahead, but you must file a *déclaration de clôture* at the local town hall *(mairie)*.

You feel like ordering a swimming pool today? No problem. You don't need building permission unless you also want to put up a pool house (in which case you may do). But you will have to lodge a *déclaration de travaux* at the *mairie,* and within one week they will post up the date from which the works may start.

You want to add on a little storage area to your property not exceeding 20m2? No building permission is necessary, but again you must lodge the *déclaration de travaux.*

You feel like resurfacing the walls of your house. Why not? No time like the present. Best get started this afternoon. You won't need any permission at all unless you are within the perimeter of a historic monument, in which case you must obtain the consent of the Historic Monuments Office, quaintly called *Monsieur l'Architecte des Bâtiments de France.*

How about a nice new greenhouse? The French for okay is *d'accord* and *d'accord* it is. You don't need any permission for this provided the greenhouse is not more than four metres in height above ground. You can even go for a whopper if you like. According to the planning code, you can make it 2,000m2 large, but I recommend you take advice before proceeding with that.

Now, how about going out for a drive on one of those French country roads lined with trees on each side. What a great pleasure! I hear you turning your engine on and revving it a bit as you set forth. I really am quite envious of you by now, but I have to say that the avenues of trees are under threat. A lot of people in France drink too much and drive too fast. When they hit a tree, people say it is the tree's fault. So there is a clamour and a movement to have them all cut down. What nonsense. We can't have one of the greatest reasons for loving France swept away for such shallow thinking as that.

# Domicile for tax purposes

## By Philippe Piedon-Lavaux          September 2003

Domicile has always been an important issue for those moving permanently to France or maintaining dual residency between France and the UK. Any international tax or estate planning needs to take this into account.

### French rules

Under the French rules and Article 4B of the French Tax Code, an individual is considered domiciled in France if for tax purposes he qualifies under any of the following tests:

• his main home is in France

• he visits France for more than 183 days per calendar year

• he carries out a professional and salaried activity in France

• he uses France as the centre of his economic interest (where his major investments are made or annual income is obtained).

For example, under Article 4B-1 of the French Tax Code, an individual can be considered from a French perspective as domiciled in France if that is where he has his permanent and habitual residence. This is the place where he or his family lives, even if he is absent some of the time but his family remains there.

(As we will see, the 1968 Double Tax Treaty between France and the UK mentions 'a' permanent home whereas the French Tax Code makes a reference to 'the' permanent home available for the taxpayer's use).

Also, under the French Tax Code, if France is the country where an individual spends most of his time, he will be considered French domiciled. It makes no difference if he occupies rented or free accommodation.

In accordance with the 4th Tax Directive (*Instruction Fiscale*) dated 1977, by staying more than six months in France an individual may be considered as having established a French domicile for tax purposes.

An individual may also qualify for French domicile if the time spent in France is more than that spent in various other countries.

Unless an individual can claim domicile elsewhere (eg the UK), he will be exposed directly to the application of the French rules (i.e. Article 4B) if he satisfies one of the above criteria.

### The double tax treaties

A double tax treaty was signed on 22 May 1968 by France and the UK in relation to income tax issues, and a further treaty on 21 June 1963 in relation to inheritance tax. For income tax purposes, one of the goals of the treaty is to avoid a scenario where an individual is deemed to be domiciled in both countries.

It is important to realise that if an individual is considered as non-domiciled in one country, say France, in accordance with the double tax treaty he will not be tax domiciled in this country, even by application of its internal rules, ie Article 4B. The double tax treaty overrides the internal rules. Also note that the definition of residency from a French perspective is approached by calendar years.

If an individual is considered domiciled in France for tax purposes in accordance with article 4B, and if he is non-domiciled in the UK for tax purposes, he will not be in a position to claim the benefit of the double tax treaty. For this to apply it is important that he is subject to an unlimited tax liability in both countries in accordance with both countries' internal rules.

Recent case law emphasises that a taxpayer who is domiciled in the French sense of the word (in accordance with Article 4B), but not fully tax domiciled in another country (e.g. ordinarily resident in the UK, but not domiciled for tax purposes), could not have the benefit of the double tax treaty with that country. The French administration requires an attestation from the local UK Inland Revenue as proof, before considering whether the double tax treaty might apply and therefore override French internal tax rules.

**Application of the double tax treaty**

When an individual is considered resident in both countries, and therefore tax domiciled in France and the UK, the double tax treaty lays out various criteria under which the domicile will be determined.

An individual shall be deemed to be a resident of the country in which he has a permanent home available to him. The French tax administration considers this to be any form of occupation of a dwelling (as a landlord or a tenant), without making any differences between a main residence or a second home. It is important that the property is a permanent home and not only available for temporary use.

In order to be considered a permanent home it would appear that the French administration may require that the home has been used for at least a year. Consequently, if an individual has a home permanently available to him in one country only, he shall be deemed to be domiciled for income tax purposes in that country only.

If he has a permanent home available to him in both countries, he shall be deemed to be a resident of the country with which his personal and economic relations are closest (the centre of vital interests).

This is probably the most difficult criteria to deal with as it requires him to go through various 'footprints' which reveal where his personal and/or professional or social links are determined. Things taken into consideration include familiar relationships, social relationships, occupation, political or cultural activities, the place where any business is conducted, the place where the tax payer used to deal and manage his affairs, the place where a bank account and financial assets are located, places where post is addressed, and the place where income tax forms are lodged.

This criteria is extremely imprecise and largely subjective. If it cannot be established that the tax payer has his centre of vital interest in one country rather than the other, and therefore the centre of vital interest cannot be determined, the individual shall be deemed to be a resident of the country in which he has a habitual residency.

We then fall under the criteria of the time physically spent in one country rather then the other. Recent case law suggests that French judges are not necessarily looking at in which place the individual has spent more time and might establish that the habitual residency is, for instance, in both countries when the taxpayer works in one country and returns to another for holidays or weekends.

If the individual has a habitual residency in both countries he shall be deemed to be a resident of the country of which he is a national.

Domicile is often difficult to establish and may need careful consideration. Reducing your time in France and also limiting the amount of 'footprints' you have in that country is more likely to influence the place where you would be deemed to be domiciled.

# Battle of the wills

By Philippe Piedon-Lavaux        January 2004

Without proper tax and estate planning French inheritance law and tax are likely to apply to those having dwellings situated in France, even if they are domiciled in the UK.

French inheritance law and tax may not only apply to the French estate, but also on assets located in other jurisdictions. A non-French purchaser should naturally be concerned about his new French property investment and also his relocation in France. Who will inherit this property or the assets left after his death? What sort of inheritance taxes are likely to apply and who will administer the estate? are some of the questions which are often not properly considered.

French law has a concept of forced heirship, which means that, as a matter of public policy, certain relatives (e.g. children, parents, and now the spouse in exceptional circumstances) are entitled to statutory rights, and therefore have the right to inherit part of the deceased's estate. Thus, these beneficiaries cannot usually be disinherited.

For example, a single purchaser with two children has to leave two-thirds of his estate to his children. With children from previous marriages this would need to be look at carefully.

### French or English will?

Some may suggest you have two separate wills dealing respectively with the UK and French estates. It is true to say that the administration of a French estate is easier to manage with a French will. But it may create problems of interpretation and conflict with an existing British will or even revoke one or the other.

It is usually easier to deal with only one will, but the solicitor or *notaire* who prepares it should ensure that the will's provisions will have full effect in any other jurisdiction. With regard to France, it is important to ensure that the will is not against any of the French inheritance statutory provisions for parents and children.

It is a question of judgement as to which is the best course of action to take, depending upon each family's circumstances.

If you decide to have a French will your French *notaire* could prepare **a)** an informal will (*testament olographe),* which is the most commonly used form in France (the only requirement is that it must be written out entirely in the hand of the testator, dated and signed by him; his signature does not need to be witnessed) or **b)** an official will *(testament authentique)*, or even **c)** a conditional gift between spouses *(donation entre époux)*, similar in many ways to a will.

The *notaire* can also prepare an international will in accordance with the Washington Convention dated 26 October 1973, and in operation in France since 1 October 1994.

French wills are registered at the French Central Index in Aix-en-Provence, which has records of 16,000,000 wills since 1974.

## Who administers the estate?

In Britain it is usually the executors (where the deceased made a will) or the administrators (where there is no will).

The common Law 'Grant of Probate' is unknown in many civil law jurisdictions, as in France. It is also important to remember that the Hague Convention dated 1 July 1985 has not yet been ratified by France, and neither does France recognise or permit the creation of trusts which are frequently inserted in UK wills.

Because French law imposes a forced heirship system, when somebody dies leaving immovable assets (eg house, land, flat) the UK executor appointed in a UK will who had power to sell a property is likely to require, in fact, the beneficiaries' consent to sell in France, when these beneficiaries have statutory rights.

## French inheritance tax

It is important to realise that insufficient planning can result in there being a taxable French estate. Whereas the proposed French Finance Act 2004 has not increased the spouse's nil rate band (76,000 euros), it is possible to obtain spouse's inheritance tax exemption in France by signing a (post) nuptial agreement.

Non-French resident individuals considering an investment in France often ask whether they should form an offshore company, use a UK company, or even use a French holding property company (usually a *Société Civile Immobilière*/SCI) to own their new investment.

There are many legal and tax aspects when acquiring and holding residential property in France through French and non-French corporate vehicles, but one of the benefits is that it may preserve the inheritance flexibility. Shares in a company are deemed to be movable assets when the shareholders are non-French domiciled. Thus they can pass according to British law under a British will.

9

## What tax is payable and can double taxation be avoided?

Double taxation relief will usually be available where there is a charge to tax in the UK and at the same time a charge to tax in France. Relief will be in accordance with the terms of the double tax agreement between the UK and France. For inheritance tax purposes the UK is a party to the double taxation agreement with France dated 21 June 1963.

Before granting relief the Revenue requires evidence that the tax has been paid in the other country by the beneficiaries or the estate.

With French Law affecting some or all of your assets you need to have legal and tax consequences explained in order to have a complete overview. Do not leave it to chance!

# Working within the law

## By Sean O'Connor    January 2004

Here is a fairly typical scenario; "I am a well-educated, presentable, intelligent English lady living in France with not quite enough to do. I would like to equip myself with an interesting occupation and earn myself some money by finding French properties for sale and introducing the owners directly to UK estate agents who will pay me a commission in England when a sale is made. I'm not interested in being involved with any French estate agents, and couldn't care a fig about French legislation governing estate agents. Anyway, since my commission will be paid in England, it's none of their business. Of course, I'm not going to pay any tax in France on my commissions. Besides, if any annoying French inspector turns up, I will just give him a flirtatious wink or two and tell him to go away."

How is yonder dame likely to get on? Not half so well as she thought.

The so-called "Hoguet Law" of 1970, named after the person who introduced it, defines the business of an estate agent as "the activity of a professional intermediary who, in exchange for a remuneration, habitually participates in operations appertaining to properties belonging to other persons where those operations consist of the purchase, sale, exchange, leasing or sub-leasing, whether furnished or unfurnished, of any properties, whether comprising buildings or not."

The said  Hoguet law provides that any person acting as such an estate agent must be the holder of a professional card (*carte professionnelle*). To obtain the card, the applicant must stump up supporting documentation as to his or her professional ability, and must produce evidence of holding a guarantee covering the repayment of any deposits or other funds lodged with the intended agent.

The lady in the above example will fall foul of the Hoguet Law because she is proposing to take part in operations appertaining  to properties owned by others. She  will be acting as an intermediary because she will be putting the owner of the French property in contact with the British agency. She will be deemed to be acting "habitually" assuming that she carries out at least two such deals per year.

Moreover, since she will be fiscally resident in France, her commissions are to be declared in France for French income tax purposes. If the commissions come up to the VAT threshold, she will also be subject to

French VAT.

One must also bear in mind that the local French estate agents are not going to find it funny to see their own work pinched from under their noses. The word will soon get round. It is almost certain that our imaginary lovely lady will be confronted with a court bailiff serving on her a summons to attend court.

She thinks that she can talk her way out of her problems, but the hole she has dug herself is deeper than she thought. Section 16 of the Hoguet Law says that the penalty will be 30,000 francs (about 4,574 euros) for a first offence and 60,000 francs ( about 9,147 euros) for a second offence and a penalty of imprisonment of six months, or either such fine or such imprisonment. Yes, she is set to hear the door of her prison cell clank shut.

It is not entirely without significance that the French word 'trou' which literally means a hole, can also mean the clink.

Let us suppose that our dear lady has tried to get round all this by using some unqualified French man to perform her acts on her behalf or by having her activities carried out by some company set up by her as a sort of façade behind which she attempts to hide.

Well, in that case, the fine bumps up to 150,000 francs (about 22,870 euros) and now she is going to be languishing in jail not for six months but for a whole two years.

So far so bad. But I do have some good news for her, as it is not so difficult as one might have first thought to get the professional card.

# Have you got what it takes?

**By Sean O'Connor    March 2004**

In a recent article I wrote about French legislation which prohibits a person from informally carrying out the functions of an estate agent in France without holding the necessary professional card (*carte professionnelle*) obtained from the local *préfecture* and which entitles the holder to practice as an estate agent.

I have been contacted by someone who has been hit with a penalty for disobeying the legislation. Briefly, he ran a website for the purpose of acting as an intermediary, to put prospective purchasers in touch with French property owners in return for a commission. He also put adverts in local newspapers in France offering to put French vendors in contact with foreign, i.e. non-French, purchasers. Although the maximum penalties can be dire, as indicated in my previous article, he was hit with a rap on the knuckles consisting of a token penalty of 3,000 euros.

How, then, can you get the professional card? It is easier than you think. In particular, if you have obtained any diploma or certificate in the UK as a result of a minimum period of two years' legal, financial or commercial studies after the *baccalaureate*, and if you have a sufficient knowledge of the French language, you are in. What is the equivalent of the *baccalaureate* for this purpose? An official at the *préfecture* of the Dordogne says this is dealt with on a case by case basis, so two good 'A' levels or three middling ones should do.

What if you haven't done any studies at all since leaving school? Good news. Provided you've got the equivalent of the *baccalaureate* (see above), then all you have to do is work full time for an estate agent in France for at least one year, whereupon you are accepted, subject to the language requirement. Alternatively, if prior to living in France you worked in an estate agent's office in the UK for two years and have a sufficient knowledge of the French language, you will be fine.

If, in the opinion of the French authorities, your UK qualifications are not up to scratch, the prefect of the geographical department where you live can require you to undergo an aptitude test, which takes place once a year in Paris, or to perform a traineeship for a period not exceeding three years.

How good does your French have to be? The answer to this, perhaps surprisingly, is that attestations stating you speak French sufficiently can be accepted. The legislation doesn't state who has to give the attestation, but the administration has discretion whether to consider the attestation reliable or not. My impression from all of this is the amount of French demanded is not very much. Alternatively, if you have got 'A' level French at grade C or higher you will be accepted.

It is important to distinguish the activities of an estate agent from certain other activities in France. The estate agent essentially acts as an intermediary putting vendor and purchaser in touch with each other. A so-called 'marchand de biens' does not do this. He or she carries on the business of buying up properties for re-sale. In accountancy terms, the properties on the books of the business are the business's stock-in-trade. The merchant pays a reduced transfer duty of 0.615% instead of the usual 4.89%, provided an undertaking is given to re-sell each property within a maximum period of four years. Such a merchant is also given special VAT treatment.

An 'agent commercial' holds an authority to sell his goods either on a commission-only basis or on a salary-plus-commission basis. He can act under the supervision of an estate agent who holds a *carte professionnelle*.

A *notaire* does the legal work involved in transferring the title, but can also engage in property transactions like an estate agent.

In conclusion, take care before you put vendors and purchasers of French properties in touch with each other for a commission. There are penalties for anyone who operates otherwise than as above.

# The buying process

By Sean O'Connor    April 2004

### The notaire

The *notaire* usually acts for both parties, but is usually chosen by the vendor. He or she has a duty to provide you with advice, but this is limited. You may have to ask relevant questions to get useful answers. You can have your own *notaire*, meaning there will be two *notaires* on the job. They have to share the fee between them so it doesn't cost you more. As you now have two cooks stirring the broth, each could blame the other for not turning the cooker on, and the whole process may take longer.

### The contract

You start with a preliminary contract called the *compromis de vente*. Once that is signed the searches are done by the *notaire*. You can include *suspensive* conditions in the contract enabling you to 'get out' if they are not concluded successfully, for example, the sale may be dependent on planning permission being granted.

There is usually a 10 % deposit. This can be lodged with the estate agent as they should have a financial guarantee against default, but it's usually best to give it to the *notaire*. If any suspensive condition is not met and the reason for this is incontrovertible, your deposit comes back to you. In doubtful cases where the vendor objects, you may have to face a court action to get your deposit back.

### The seven-day law

You have to be served with a copy of the contract, bearing your signature and the vendor's, with a notice giving you seven days to cancel. The notice can either be posted or handed to you. If the notice is handed to you before the vendor has signed the contract, the notice is not valid. The seven days run from the day following the date on which you receive the notice. If you do nothing, then after the seven days the contract becomes binding (subject to the *suspensive* conditions and successful conveyancing).

If you are not buying residential premises, for example you are buying a building plot, you do not have the right of cancellation.

### The searches

The *notaire* conducts the conveyancing searches. Be aware that these will not always show up development projects afoot, unless they are actually on your property. Thus if a six-lane highway is about to be built alongside but not on your property, the search will not necessarily tell you this. It is sensible to make additional local enquiries in appropriate cases.

### The cadastral plan

This plan, kept by the local tax office and also available in the *mairie,* shows every plot of land in the local area. The land you are buying is purchased with reference to it. It is a good idea to see the plan to check what you are buying. The initial contract is often sent out without the plan. You should ask for it.

### The local land registry

This is not a land registry in the British sense, it is called the mortgages office in French. Title deeds and mortgage deeds are entered in the registry, but title does not result from registration. The purpose of the register is to give notice to the public of the ownership of land and of the mortgages on it. Such registration is called in French 'publicité foncière', which has nothing at all to do with publicity in the English sense.

The *notaire* will search the registry to check the vendor has not somehow whopped on a hefty mortgage against the property in a sum greater than the purchase price. If he has, you can rescind. If a mortgage has been granted but has not been entered on the registry, you are not liable for it.

### The deed of sale

The deed of sale *(acte de vente)* conveys the title to you. The deed has to be prepared by a French *notaire,* whose fees and costs, in the order of around 7%, must be paid. These include the transfer duties which currently amount to 5.09 % of the price.

If you are unable to visit the *notaire's* office to sign the *acte,* you can give power of attorney to someone else, for example, you can authorise a clerk in the *notaire's* office to sign on your behalf.

After the deed has been signed, you don't see it again. It goes to the local land registry for registration and for payment of the transfer duties. Then it is sent back to the *notaire,* who holds it permanently in his files. This document constitutes your title. You will receive a certified copy of it, normally sent to you about three months after signing the *acte.*

If you have read this far, you deserve a GCSE in French conveyancing. However you may note some important topics have not been dealt with. For example, what about adverse rights of way? What about your own mortgage on the property if you want one? What about boundaries and planning permissions? Watch this space.

# The French way Part I

## By Philippe Piedon-Lavaux    May 2004

Buying property in France can be an intimidating experience. This is a stressful time as purchasers are dealing not only with a foreign legal system but also a foreign language, and a legal language at that. It's complicated, even for the French! So who are the 'actors' on this legal stage, and what are the different 'acts'?

### The French notaire

He (or she) is a public official appointed by the French Ministry of Justice. The *notaire* does not act in the same way as a solicitor. His duties towards his clients are different. Do not expect him to represent you in the same way as you are used to in the UK. For example, inadequate professional service is a matter of negligence in France. Delays and lack of responsiveness are still frequent. However, the profession is adapting due to pressure from other legal professions and consumers.

### The estate agent

Estate agents selling French property operate on both sides of the Channel. They owe a professional duty of care to their clients and you should always check they are registered. Obtain answers to any questions in writing from your estate agent.

### The solicitor

Solicitors can check the legal documentation and offer helpful independent assistance, from both a tax and a legal point of view throughout the transaction. They are independent and therefore you will receive impartial advice.

### Preliminary queries

### French inheritance position

You should consider the impact of French inheritance rules before committing yourself to a property purchase. French rules of inheritance provide statutory rights to certain relatives (eg children or parents). It is important to ascertain that you will be in a position to transfer the property in the way you would like. The French rules provide some flexibility, but do not under estimate the statutory regulations.

### French tax position

You should consider the tax position before moving to France, especially if you intend to relocate permanently, as there are likely to be taxes on your world wide assets. The French tax system does not provide the same tax-free threshold and without proper tax planning the exercise might become expensive.

## Property description

Properties in France are described under a plot number and we advise you to get a map showing existing boundaries. Vendors do not guarantee these boundaries and you will need to ascertain (with a map or with the help of a land surveyor) where the boundaries lie.

## Contents and fixtures

The definition of fixtures and fittings is different in France and we would recommend an inventory of the contents, fixtures and fittings you intend to keep. French contracts do not usually include such an inventory, with the exception in some circumstances of a contents list. A more detailed inventory is advisable to avoid any surprises!

## Planning

It is essential to know whether the vendors have done any work on the property requiring planning permission. If none was granted, you could face a claim for damages. The local authorities might even be entitled to knock down works done without permission.

## Surroundings

The property's immediate environment is a matter of frequent concern as it might attract disturbance (noise, pollution or obstruction of views). It is advisable to investigate this with the local authorities and to check whether any planning applications have been granted on neighbouring properties, and also what neighbours would be entitled to apply for. It will also give some indication of what you would be able to do with your property.

## Works and improvements

If works have been done, we advise you get confirmation as to whether a professional has carried them out. If this is the case the work should be covered by a 10-year professional guarantee. In addition the French rules of capital gains tax which came into force on 1 January 2004 provide a limited allowance for those who have carried out works themselves or with a non-registered builder.

## Drainage

Investigate whether the property is connected to the public drainage system or to an individual septic tank. If the property is connected to a septic tank, it is important to access whether the system meets required health and safety standards.

**Health and safety**

Where applicable you will need surveys for asbestos, lead painting and termites prior to exchanging contracts (in some areas it is compulsory for the vendor to provide and pay for the survey). In addition, should you feel there might be a flooding risk you should contact local authorities who can confirm whether this is the case or not. Isolated dwellings in the south of France might need confirmation that they are sufficiently provided with water.

**Conveyancing process**

In France the vendor and purchaser are required to exchange contracts (*compromis de vente*) at the early stages of the process after the offer has been accepted (an offer can be made either verbally or in writing).

The purchaser signs the initial contract without necessarily receiving the results of the searches, surveys or even confirmation that finances are in place. Protection of the purchaser when 'signing blind' is provided by 'let-out' clauses (*conditions suspensive*). The most frequent let-out clauses cover the existence of any covenant, rights of way, outstanding mortgage, third parties rights and finance. If one of these conditions is not met the purchaser can pull out of the purchase and receive a full refund of their deposit. If all conditions are met or waived the purchasers will have to complete.

**Exchange of contracts**

The most frequently used initial contract is the **compromis de vente**, a binding contract. If one of the parties does not want to proceed, the other one can start proceedings generally, apply for specific performance and ask the court to enforce it. The party in breach who refused to complete will have to pay damages and all the related costs and in certain circumstances, depending on the clauses in the contract, a penalty.

**The deposit**

The frequently required deposit is 10%. This is usually payable upon the exchange of the *compromis de vente*. The amount can be reduced if the parties agree. It is extremely unlikely that a deposit will attract interest. The deposit will be considered as a payment on account should completion take place.

**Cooling-off period**

Purchasers have the benefit of a seven-day cooling-off period. It is advisable to check with either your agent or lawyer when the first day of the cooling-off period starts. The cooling-off period gives the purchaser the right to withdraw, for any reason.

**Searches, surveys and finance**

Searches will be organised by the *notaire* and the result disclosed closer to completion of the final contract. It is unusual to have a survey clause in France and we recommend any surveys are organised prior to signing the initial contract. For those who do not have their finance in place it is possible to sign a contract subject to finance. Delays for getting finance in place in France should not be under estimated, and it is therefore advisable to consider a realistic completion date.

**Completion**

The *notaire* will confirm when he is ready to get the parties to sign the final deed. There is usually no penalty for late completion in France and we recommend you do not book any travel arrangements, removals or lettings unless the completion date has been confirmed. *Notaires d*o not accept banker's drafts or cheques from non-French based banks. They ask for the funds to be in their client account prior to completion or a banker's draft from a French based bank. The purchasers will be required to pay the balance of the funds due, plus stamp duty and legal fees and also any agent's fees (if any).

This is a limited list and we strongly recommend those not familiar with the French system seek advice.

# The French way Part II

## By Philippe Piedon-Lavaux    June 2004

For inheritance or tax purposes some buyers structure their French property purchase through a French company Some recent developments should be taken into consideration for the running of these companies or for any future investors.

It has been suggested that the UK Inland Revenue might take the view that an SCI is in English law to be considered more as a company than as a partnership. The result may be that the Revenue assess the shareholders to a benefit in kind charge on the availability of rent-free accommodation. This is because the shareholders may have influence over the SCI in terms of management decisions (such as making improvements) and be deemed as shadow directors of the SCI. Directors are liable as employees to income tax charges on taxable benefits received from the company.

Thus, we would advise signing a declaration of trust saying that the SCI holds the property as nominee for your shareholders in order to avoid any benefit in kind liability under the UK income tax regime. If the shareholders or beneficiaries are resident somewhere else than in the UK then the likely tax treatment of such a benefit in the relevant jurisdiction should be considered. The taxable benefit in the UK would be calculated by subtracting the first £75,000 of value from the value of the house and applying the rate of 7% on the balance as being deemed rented value. Income tax would be levied at your marginal rate on this figure.

We would also advise that you appoint a French-resident board of directors to avoid the SCI being considered as UK based for tax purposes. If effective control and decision making does not reside in France, the UK Inland Revenue may decide that the SCI should be subject to UK corporation tax. In addition, the French Inland Revenue may also decide that the SCI should be considered as a non-French based company, automatically subject to French corporation tax (Subject to any allowance provided under the double tax treaty).

### Succession problems

While SCIs are considered to be an attractive vehicle by avoiding the French compulsory succession rules applicable to French property, there is a possible, although unlikely, outcome that the interaction between the UK and French rules might mean that the use of an SCI does not avoid these compulsory French succession rules, if a declaration of trust is used.

In that event there is a possibility that the SCI will be disregarded by French succession law, as the property will under UK law be effectively owned by the individual rather than the company and accordingly will devolve under French law, as it is immovable property in France.

That would depend upon someone making a claim as such and exploiting the interaction between the UK and the French succession laws to their advantage, but you may feel the risk of such a claim being made is insignificant compared to the possibility of an income tax charge being applied during your lifetime. If you think there is a very real risk, there is a solution, which involves the use of a life interest trust instead of a simple declaration of trust.

### Double tax treaties (DTT)

Anyone moving or buying in France should seek advice and make a review of his potential tax liability. Domicile in France is not used in the British sense of the term, but is broadly equivalent to the British concept of residence, which determines liability for income tax, inheritance tax, capital gains tax and wealth tax in some cases.

### French tax rules

Under Article 4 B of the French Tax Code an individual is deemed to be considered domiciled in France if he satisfies any of the following tests:

- his main home is in France
- or he visits France for more than 183 days per calendar year
- or he carries out a professional or salaried activity in France
- or he uses France as the centre of his economic interests (where his major investments are made or annual income is obtained).

Unless an individual can claim domicile elsewhere (e.g. the UK) he will be exposed directly to the application of the French rules (ie Article 4 B) if he satisfies one of the above criteria.

A DTT was signed on 22 May 1968 between France and the UK in relation to income and capital gains tax issues, and another DTT on 21 June 1963 in relation to inheritance tax. If an individual is considered as non-domiciled in one country, say France, in accordance *with* the DTT, he will not be tax domiciled in that country even by application of its internal rules (Article 4 B). The DTT thus overrides internal rules.

For the benefit of the DTT to apply an individual must be subject to an unlimited tax liability in both countries in accordance with both countries internal rules. Recent case law emphasises that a taxpayer who was domiciled in the French sense of the word (in accordance with Article 4 B), but who is not fully tax domiciled in another country (e.g. ordinarily resident in the UK but not domiciled for tax purposes), could not have the benefit of the DTT with that country.

When an individual is considered as a resident in both countries, and therefore deemed to be tax domiciled in France and resident in the UK, the double tax treaty lays out various tests under which his domicile/residence will be determined. An individual shall be deemed to be domiciled/resident of the country in which he has a permanent home available to him. The French tax administration considers this to be any form of occupation of a dwelling, without differentiating between a main residence, or a second home. If he has a permanent home available to him in both countries he shall be deemed to be domiciled/resident of the country with which his personal and economic relations are closest (centre of vital interests).

This is probably the most difficult criterion to deal with as it requires him to go through various steps, which would reveal where his personal and/or professional social links are. These steps give indications of domicile/residency and can be thought of as 'footprints' in the country If the individual has a habitual residency in both countries then he shall be deemed to be domiciled/resident of the country of which he is a national.

Among various taxes, individuals who own a property in France should consider in particular the following.

Any income arising in France from a French source has to be disclosed to the French Revenue and taxed in France. In this case, an income tax form would have to be lodged before 30 April each year. Under Article 164(c) individuals who are not resident in France for tax purposes, but have residential property there available to them, are liable to French income tax on the basis that they receive an income equal to, but not less than, three times the rental value of the property, unless they have other French income exceeding this amount.

Residents of countries having a double tax treaty with France (such as the UK) are exempt from such assessments but residents of countries which do not have such a treaty (e.g. Jersey or any tax haven) are not.

Regardless of their nationality persons not resident in France are taxed on their income from French sources on, for example, income from French sources such as letting income which will be taxed at 25% minimum, unless the taxpayer can invoke a reduced tax liability with regard to his world-wide income elsewhere. Salaries, pensions or annuities are also taxable for non-domiciled individuals in France although various exemptions are available.

On resale a person owning a property in France will be liable for French capital gains tax (CGT) at the rate of 16% if not French tax domiciled (in the French sense of the word) but European domiciled. There are some tax allowances and exemptions available depending on the circumstances. A property-bought or subject to VAT is also likely to attract VAT on resale if sold within five years after completion.

From 30 March 2004 an individual must appoint a CGT representative agent (costs would be incurred) unless the sale price is less than 150,000 euros.

In any event, the tax implications for both income or holding assets should be looked at.

# Local taxes

**By Sean O'Connor    July 2004**

There are two local taxes in France, land tax *(taxe fonciere)* and the habitation tax *(taxe d'habitation)*.

The land tax is charged on houses and land. Barns, stables, attics, storage rooms and cellars are exempt. New constructions are normally exempt for a period of two years, but the local commune can resolve to strike out this exemption wholly or partly.

If the property is your principal residence, you are a low income person and you are aged over 65, you get 100 euros off your land tax bill. If in the same circumstances, you are aged over 75, you are totally exempt from the land tax.

There is a complicated method of calculating low income for these purposes. I won't go into it but, for example, if you are 75-plus and are married, with no children, vou will be exempt from land tax if your joint income does not exceed 10,993 euros.

The amount of the land tax is calculated like rates used to be calculated in the UK. You take the so-called cadastral letting value multiplied by the rate fixed by the local authority.

If you let the property out, the person who has to pay the land tax is you, in all circumstances.

When you purchase a property, the land tax is split, for the calendar year considered, on a time basis.

I turn now to the habitation tax. When you buy a property this is not split on a time basis. The vendor pays it for the whole of the year during which you purchase.

The habitation tax is payable if your property is habitable, whether you live in it or whether anyone else lives in it or not. If it is not habitable, you can get the tax vacated to use the English fiscal expression (*degreve* in French).

If the property is your principal residence and you let it furnished, you pay the habitation tax, not the tenant. If the property is not your principal residence and you let it furnished, the tenant has to pay the habitation tax. If you let the property unfurnished, the tenant pays the habitation tax.

If the property is your principal residence, you get a certain amount off for persons being supported by you, including children up to the age of 18 or children up to the age of 25 who have signed up papers to be fiscally reattached to their parents, and your own parents if aged over 70 and if they are on low incomes.

If you are on a low income and aged over 60, or a widow or widower whatever your age and are on a low income, you are totally exempt from the habitation tax but only if the property is your principal residence.

If you are not quite cash-strapped enough to be a low-income person, but are nevertheless still hard up, you can get a certain amount off. Your whole position is considered as at 1 January each year.

As regards both the habitation and land tax, the demands for the year considered are sent out in the autumn. Thus for the year 2004, the demand will not normally be sent out until September or October. The taxes are payable within 30 days. If you don't pay within the due time, the amount of the tax gets bumped up 10%. You also have to pay interest for delay at 0.75% per month. In an extreme case of non-compliance, the administration could obtain a charging order on your property and repossess.

Education is financed centrally, not locally in France. So normally the habitation tax and land tax combined will come to a bit less than UK council tax.

# Can't even give it away

By Sean O'Connor    August 2004

Let's call him Mr Green. He owns a property in France which just happens to be his principal asset. He is in somewhat ailing health and may not be in this world for much longer. He has two adult children, who are fortunately both doing very well. He is married for the second time, his wife is younger than him and he would like to transfer the French property into her name, so after he has gone she will not want in her old age.

Of course Mr Green could simply make a French will leaving one-quarter of the property to his wife absolutely and three-quarters in life interest with remainder in those three-quarters to his two children in equal shares. This means that, supposing the property to be worth £100,000, if (after Mr Green's death) Mrs Green decides to sell the property, she must hand over £75,000 to the children, minus the value of her life interest in 75% of the property. If she is aged between 70 and 80 when she decides to sell, the value of her life interest will be 30%.

However, Mr Green wants his wife to be free of any future entanglement with the children, so he would like simply to give the whole property to her now. Maitre Dupont, the French notary, reacts by saying that

under French law a deed of gift between spouses is always revocable so that during Mr Green's lifetime Mrs Green's position remains precarious in the sense that he might revoke his deed of gift at any time. However, French law refers such matters to the personal law of the spouses, in this case English law since both of them are of British nationality, normally resident in England. Under English law, the deed of gift can be rendered irrevocable and French law accepts this. Hence Mr Green's deed of gift will, in his particular case, be irrevocable in France.

Maitre Dupont then throws another spanner in the works. He says that the proposed deed of gift is designed to strip Mr Green's two children of their compulsory right to two-thirds of the French property (one-third each). They can attack the deed of gift as soon as Mr Green has died. Therefore the gift should not be proceeded with. He is against it, and will not agree to sign it up.

In response to that, Mr Green's well-off and amiable children then say they are willing to appear as parties in the proposed deed of gift of the French property to their step-mother. Surely, they say, this sorts that one out.

No it won't, replies Maitre Dupont. For under French law, they are not allowed, prior to their father's death, to sign any papers purporting to sort out what is to happen to their father's French property after he has died. In France this is called a pact concerning future estate, which the French civil code expressly prohibits. Mr Green's plan is therefore stymied. He is forced to say to his wife: "The deed of gift is off, dear".

So can't Mr Green sort it all out simply by selling the property to his wife? The answer is yes  provided the couple have enough money in the kitty to put through Maitre Dupont's client account the sale price, plus Dupont's fees and costs amounting to approximately 7% of the price, plus any French capital gains tax that may be payable. Unfortunately, they do not have the necessary funds available.

Well then, what about Mr Green putting the French property into the name of a French civil real-estate company, that is to say a *societe civile immobiliere* or SCI for short? The shares in the SCI would rank as moveables. French and English law are agreed in saying that moveables devolve in accordance with the law of the domicile. Mr and Mrs Green live in England. So Mr Green can simply leave all of the shares in the SCI to Mrs Green under his English will. Sounds good.

Nevertheless, we are not home and dry. For, firstly, putting the property into the name of an SCI is an event triggering French capital gains tax. Secondly, the fees for establishing the SCI are significant in amount. Thirdly, there may be some potential fiscal problems in the UK concern ing holding a French property through an SCI. These are matters for another time.

In view of all this, Mr Greer goes back to square one. He will make a French will after all. It is easy, costs little, keeps things simple, and gives Mr and Mrs Green most of what they want. All of this supports the old adage where there's a will, there's a way.

# Joint ownership

## By Philippe Piedon–Lavaux    August 2004

The French Property Exhibition, which takes place in September, will probably reveal the continued interest in French properties. The most common concerns for those buying with friends and family will relate to tax planning and estate planning.

Often UK individuals buying with friends and family wonder how they should purchase their French property and also when they should put a suitable structure in place. It seems appropriate therefore to remind people of various ways in which they could proceed.

### French inheritance law

First bear in mind that French inheritance law will apply to the French property bought in individuals' names, even if the owners remain domiciled in the UK.

It may be appropriate to warn those who have children (especially under 18 years of age), that French inheritance law imposes a forced heirship system. It follows that when somebody dies leaving immovable assets in France, the deceased's children (or, if no children, any surviving parents) have to inherit part of the deceased's estate and cannot be disinherited. Consent to the sale of the property owned by such children is necessary and you will appreciate that the situation could be even more difficult when the children entitled are from a previous relationship.

### French tenancy agreement

By purchasing in tenancy in common (ie *en indivision)*, the property is shared between the purchasers according to their financial contribution. Each of the purchasers owns a share of the house and the surviving partner will not automatically inherit the predeceased partner's share. There can be an agreement between the tenants in common *(co-indivisaires)* called *'convention d'indivision'*. This agreement must be in writing and will last for a period of five years, and is renewable.

This convention will be set out in a deed and will govern matters such as rights of first refusal; the proportion of contribution to the purchase monies; the rights of the manager responsible for representing all the co-owners; creditors' rights; management and votes; possession of the property; bank accounts etc. The *'convention d'indivision'* should be supplemented by house rules providing for the day-to-day running of the property, period of occupancy etc.

The statutory legal rights operate on the death of a co-owner, but the deed can provide that the surviving co-owner(s) will be able to purchase the deceased's share. When there is co-ownership between individuals, in the event of a disagreement over the sale of the property the party wishing to sell can compel the other party to sell his/her share without any further condition.

Consequently, during the lifetime of the co-owners *'en indivision'* one party can claim and force a sale of the property without the consent of the other. An exception to this rule is when the property is used as the family's main residence and if the surviving spouse does not wish to sell he/she can petition the court to obtain a priority to keep and purchase the house.

**The use of a company**

Also remember that by structuring the purchase via a company the French property could be governed by another inheritance law such as UK inheritance law, as long as the shareholders remain UK domiciled from a French point of view. Therefore UK investors have the opportunity to put their French property under UK inheritance law by setting up a company or using an existing one. A director will be appointed which will ease the management of the property between the various users.

Very often UK purchasers realise just before completing the final title deed *(acte de vente)* in the *notaire's* office that they should have put the property under another structure (i..e a company).

It might be recommended from a tax point of view to hold the French property with a French company *(societe civile immobiliere/SCI)*. There are issues both in France and in the UK for those using such companies, which would need to be considered before buying and we would recommend that you take detailed advice.

**The 'clause tontine'**

It is possible to purchase a French property and insert a joint tenancy agreement or survivorship clause *(tontine)* into the deed of sale between the various co-owners. The effect of this clause is to transfer the ownership of the property automatically to the survivor(s) on the death of the first joint owner. This will override the French statutory inheritance rules on the first death.

The survivor(s) will therefore be deemed, upon the death of the first, to be the legal owner (s) of the whole of the property, without any of it forming a part of the deceased's estate for the application of the laws of succession. (However, from an inheritance tax standpoint, the deceased's share will continue to be considered part of the deceased's estate and therefore taxed accordingly (i.e. either French inheritance tax or stamp duty, depending on the circumstances).

A survivorship clause will only be valid if the parties have contributed equally to the purchase price and have similar life expectancies. Bear in mind that the co-owners cannot sever the scheme without all co-owners' consent.

**French nuptial agreement**

More and more UK spouses are purchasing in this manner. It is now widely known that adopting a French nuptial agreement could prove of great advantage to UK couples buying in France. All French properties acquired by a husband and wife will be deemed to be communal and belong to a common fund *(la communaute universelle)* administered jointly.

The entire common fund accrues to the survivor without French inheritance tax. French tax-domiciled individuals who are subject to French inheritance tax on their worldwide assets may maximise the tax position by also including assets other than just the French property. In this way they will not only avoid and override the effects of the well-known French inheritance laws on the first death, but also improve the estate planning position as transfer of assets between spouses will be exempt of French inheritance tax.

French Law should be flexible enough to accommodate your wishes. But don't leave it to the future as things put on hold usually remain as they are or cannot be reverted. It is usually less expensive to put the right structure in place before completing on a house purchase.

# Contract off

**By Sean O'Connor    September 2004**

If you have signed a contract for the purchase of a residential property in France, you must be given a notice (by hand or post) advising you that you have a right to cancel within seven days. The seven-day period runs from the day following the date on which you receive the notice. At the same time as the notice, you must also receive a copy of the contract *(compromis de vente)* bearing your and the vendor's signatures.

The notice can be handed to you by the estate agent when you sign the contract, provided they also hand you a copy of the contract bearing both signatures. If the notice is handed to you together with a copy of the contract without the vendor's signature it is not valid.

If the notice bearing both signatures is to be posted, it must be sent by recorded delivery with proof of receipt, or by any other means providing equivalent certainty for determining the date on which you receive the notice.

Alternatively, the estate agent may send you the proposed contract, not yet signed by you, together with the notice, in the form of an acknowledgement of receipt to be signed by you. If the vendor has already signed the contract, then when you've signed it and the acknowledgement of receipt of the notice, the whole exercise will have been satisfactorily carried out because there will have been a brief moment when you had a contract signed by both parties in . front of you.

If the estate agent sends the receipt of notice and draft contract without it having been signed by the vendor, the exercise isn't valid because there was never a moment when you saw a text of the contract signed by both parties. In other words, it is not sufficient for you to sign the acknowledgement of the receipt of the notice and for the vendor to sign the contract afterwards.

If you want to implement your cancellation right, you should normally do so by sending a letter by recorded delivery with proof of receipt to the person who sent it to you, doing so within the seven days. The fact that your letter arrives after the seven days have expired doesn't matter. Alternatively, you can exercise the cancellation right by any other means presenting equivalent proof as to the date on which you sent your advice of cancellation.

If the notice is not sent to you at all, your right to cancel remains intact.

However, instead of sending you the notice together with a copy of the contract bearing the signature of both parties, the *notaire* can send you the text of the proposed draft deed together with a notice giving you seven days to decide whether to go ahead with the transaction or not. In this case, of course, the draft deed doesn't bear any signatures. If you do decide to proceed after having received such a notice, the text of the deed as subsequently signed must not materially differ from the text sent for you to consider during the seven-day period.

You can send the deposit during the seven-day period provided you send it to a qualified estate agent or *notaire* only. If you subsequently exercise your cancellation right, the person who received the deposit must send it back to you within 21 days from the day following the date on which you exercised your cancellation right.

You do not need to give any reason for exercising your right to cancel. You can simply say you just don't want the property any more.

(Note: the cancellation right only applies to contracts for residential properties. It does not apply to the purchase of a building-plot.)

# French property leases

**By Philippe Piedon-Lavaux    October 2004**

Leases, which apply to dwellings, farming land or commercial properties, are strictly regulated in France. Anyone who purchases a property subject to such a lease should take legal advice and get an explanation of the legal consequences of having a tenant.

### Commercial lease

Commercial leases are regulated under the Lease Act dated 30 September 1953. They gained an increased interest for those investing in leaseback properties with the benefit of a VAT rebate scheme.

To have the benefit of the VAT rebate scheme, entering into a commercial lease is necessary.

At the end of the first lease period you will be required to continue to lease the property at your tenant's request.

If you wish to repossess the property you will have to get the tenant's consent to cancel the lease at the end of the initial lease period. As your lease is regulated by the Commercial Lease Act, your tenant will be able to claim for loss of income, and in the event of a disagreement, a French court will then fix the indemnity due to the tenant in accordance with the loss. Any cancellation for the renewal of the commercial lease by the tenant will be void if signed prior to the signature of the lease contract.

Your tenant could pull out from the lease at any time, or decide not to renew your lease, which will not only wind up the lease contract but also attract the repayment of VAT if you are not in a position to sign a new commercial lease with another tenant.

Again, under the French Commercial Act, your tenant has an automatic right to renew his lease unless you give him notice, but you may face, as indicated above, a claim for loss of income.

There are other issues which would need to be looked at such as the right to increase the rent or the possibility for the tenant to sell or sub-lease the property In addition the contract should also indicate for example who will be responsible for the local taxes and the renewal of the contents.

### Farming lease

The Lease Act 1946, which regulates most farming leases, increased the minimum length of a lease contract. The tenant is entitled to an automatic renewal of the lease as well as a pre-emption right should the property be sold. Contractual freedom was affected by the need to establish economic stability for farmers.

The minimum length of the lease is nine years. There are other longer periods available which might in fact be beneficial; the 25-year lease contains, for example, an exemption to the automatic renewal right. In principle the sale of the lease or sublease are forbidden, however, there is a right to transfer (subject to conditions) the lease to either the spouse or certain relatives. This also applies in the case of death.

**Property lease**

There is a major difference for those letting their property furnished and those who prefer to lease it empty.

When leasing a furnished property the parties involved are free to decide under which conditions it should be organised. They will be regulated by the Civil Code.

However, the French Property Act dated 29 July 1998 contains some dispositions with regard to landlords leasing furnished properties.

In accordance with article L.632-1 to L.632-3 of the Construction and Habitation Code, any tenants of a furnished property being used as a dwelling are protected when the landlord leases more than four furnished units. For example, the tenants should have a minimum one-year written lease. This contract is automatically renewable for a similar period. The landlord can change the lease conditions at the end of the lease only if he gives notice of the new conditions to the tenants three months before the end of the lease period. The landlord can terminate the lease by giving notice three months before its term, but only for a valid motive. The tenant can end the lease at any time after one month's notice.

As far as unfurnished properties are concerned they are mainly regulated by the Lease Act dated 6 July 1989 and 21 July 1994. These rules are compulsory, with the overall aim to protect the tenant who is considered as the weakest contractual party.

The contract needs to be in writing and should contain the parties' details, the lease period, the description of the property which is being leased and any equipment/contents, the amount of rent and how it should be paid or amended. Finally, the amount of the deposit should be indicated with a maximum of two months' rent. We would strongly recommend an inventory, otherwise the property would be deemed to be in a good state. When the property is located in a block or condominium the landlord should provide a copy of the rules which are applicable.

The landlord is obliged to deliver a property in a good state of repair and also ensure a peaceful environment. The lease would be for a minimum period of three years unless the landlord has a need for the property for family or professional reasons. In these circumstances the lease cannot be for any less than a year. Corporate structures are entitled to a six-year lease.

The landlord can recover the property at the end of the lease period or by giving at least six months' notice, but only for one of the following three reasons: **a)** for living there, **b)** for selling the property, **c)** for any other legitimate or serious reason. The tenant can end the lease at any time after giving three months' notice which can be reduced to one month, for example in the case of a career move.

It is imperative that anyone intending to buy a property which is already leased or who wishes to let a property should obtain and look at in detail the lease documentation. Detailed advice should be taken prior to becoming bound into any lease contract. Should you experience a breach of contract for non-payment of the rent, for example, experience proves that it is likely to take time and effort in France to repossess an empty property. French courts do not usually order expulsions during the winter season. One might consider taking insurance or additional guarantees to protect against such eventualities.

# Plan of action

## By Sean O'Connor    October 2004

I come back to outline planning permission because some clients have been having difficulties with this. Old hands, this will be a refresher and brush-up. New readers, note carefully.

Outline planning permission is called a *certificat d'urbanisme*. Who applies for it? It can be the *notaire,* but he may farm out the job to a land surveyor (géomètre) or it can be your architect if you have one. It is important to ascertain that the application has actually been lodged. The decision should be handed down within two months of demand, but often it takes three months or even longer. So an appropriate lead-time should be laid down in the contract.

A majority, but by no means all communes in France have a land development plan. You had better learn some local lingo here. It is called *le plan* or POS for short. The commune will be divided up into areas within which, very briefly, development is or is not permitted or is only permitted with restrictions. It is useful to obtain the rules governing the zone in which your property is located.

The POS will have a COS meaning *coefficient d'occupation des sols* or land occupation coefficient. Assuming your property is located in a constructible area, the surface area of your plot multiplied by the coefficient minus the surface area of the existing buildings will give you the surface area available for further construction. Thus if your plot has 1,000m2 and the COS is 0.5, and the existing buildings are 300m2, you can construct a further 200m2.

The constructible surface area is called the *surface hors oeuvres nette or* SHON for short.

The measurements are taken from outside the walls. This is the meaning of *hors* (outside) *oeuvres* (works). All floors are included. Thus if the existing building has three floors, all three count, and if you want to build an extension with two floors, both count. Uninhabitable attic space, uninhabitable basement space, balconies and terraces are not included. Garages are not included. Barns, sheds and other similar outbuildings are not included.

Thus the existing SHON only appertains to the existing habitable surface area, and the residual SHON only appertains to future possible habitable surface area, excluding the items just mentioned. In doubtful cases, it is prudent to ask a land surveyor or your architect to confirm that the *certificat d'urbanisme* in fact allows you to do what you wish to do. You only compulsorily need an architect if the SHON that you intend to construct exceeds 170m2. Normally, of course, the outline planning permission must be followed by a building permit *(permis de construire)*.

The *certificat d'urbanisme* is valid for one year from date of issue, automatically renewable for a second year, provided you lodge your application for renewal within 10 months within the date of issue. The *certificat* may be subject to conditions, which should be carefully studied.

# Caring and sharing

**By Sean O'Connor    November 2004**

Co-ownership (*copropriété*) is the legal relationship you enter into when you purchase a flat in a block in France. Co-ownership is also sometimes used where there are facilities in common, such as a swimming pool on a housing estate. In what follows, I shall concentrate on the block of flats situation.

Co-ownership is governed by the Law of 10 July 1965 (as amended). A deed divides the block into lot numbers which refer to the flats, storage rooms and parking spaces. You purchase one or more lot numbers and compulsorily become a member of an association of co-owners. Considered collectively, the association owns the land on which the building stands. Notionally, each lot number carries a portion of the common parts of the building, e.g. the corridors, and also of the land. That proportion determines your voting rights at meetings of the association.

Your title to your flat thus consists of your ownership of the lot numbers concerned, nothing else.

The association has a manager (*le syndic*), who may be one of the members or an outside entity such as an estate agency. The manager generally runs the block, in the sense of heating, lighting and cleaning common areas. A service charge is voted through at the annual general meeting. The meeting appoints the manager and can dismiss him. Certain large-scale associations of co-owners also have a supervisory committee (*le conseil syndical*), which keeps the manager up to the mark.

A set of rules governs the association (*le règlement de copropriété*) with which you and other members have to comply. The rules of your particular association will be similar to but not necessarily identical to those of other associations, bearing in mind they always have to comply with the 1965 Law. Thus you must live in your flat

'bourgeoisement', meaning in an upright manner, and your lifestyle within the flat must be 'de bonne vie et moeurs', ie proper and correct. Some 'non-bourgeois' activities are expressly prohibited, for example, no throwing of objects out of the windows and no cluttering up the common areas. Dogs and cats are tolerated, but other animals are prohibited.

Proposals for any heavy repairs, i.e. repairs to the structure, are submitted to the AGM, which votes on them.

Normally, the association insures the building against fire, but you need insurance covering your personal effects and also such matters as water leaking from your flat to the one below, or a fire burning down the whole block being attributable to the negligence of yourself, your family or guests.

In England, until now, flats in a block have been held under long leases, each with covenants to repair and behave properly. The freeholder pays the ground rents, levies a service charge, carries out the repairs and enforces the good behaviour provisions. However, since 27 September 2004, it is possible for a block in England to be 'commonhold', which is similar to French co-ownership, but the following differences can usefully be noted.

Firstly, the rules governing commonhold are much more complicated than the provisions contained in the French law on co-ownership. Secondly, under the commonhold system, each flat owner has a registered title issued by HM Land Registry, such that the title to the flat is guaranteed by the State. It does not simply depend on being a member of the commonhold association.

Under the commonhold scheme, there is a community statement, which is roughly the equivalent of the co-ownership rules in the French system. The commonhold association has directors who broadly speaking fulfil the same function as the manager of a French co-ownership association.

I have been told that commonhold is the first new manner of holding land to be introduced since the 14th century. It could be said that English law has caught up with French law about 40 years late!

# Cross-border relationships

By Jenny Freeman and Philippe Piédon-Lavaux
November 2004

In these days of greater social and economic mobility, it is not surprising that more and more British citizens are deciding to set up homes abroad and notably in other EU member states such as France and Spain. This may be for work or personal reasons, or both. Additionally, there are now greater possibilities for relationship and family formation between individuals from different nations.

By way of response to this greater mobility and to social trends, a European regulation known as Brussels II was implemented on 1 March 2001 to deal with certain family matters including divorce. The aim of this treaty was officially to address "differences between certain national rules governing jurisdiction and enforcement [which] hamper the free movement of persons and the sound operation of the internal market". In other words, Brussels II aims to remove legal, social and economic obstacles to the freedom of movement of individuals of European member states. Today, Brussels II applies to all EU member states (except Denmark), including the 10 accession states.

So what is the practical impact of Brussels II on a couple or a spouse wishing to get divorced where there is a European element to their relationship as referred to above?

One might easily imagine that if one were married in England or Wales then the courts of those countries would be the only ones to deal with any divorce suit. Under Brussels II, this will not always be the case. In fact, more than one member state of the European Union may have jurisdiction to deal with the case. Jurisdiction and the forum in which the divorce case will be heard depends on two quite complicated and different legal concepts of 'habitual residence' and 'domicile'. In broad terms, the courts of a member state can accept jurisdiction where one of the parties habitually resides in, is a national of or, in certain circumstances, is domiciled in that member state. It should be noted however that legal advice should be sought on the meaning of these terms and further, that neither party can commence proceedings in a country until they have lived there for at least six months.

Where proceedings are commenced in two separate European member states, both of which legally have jurisdiction, the party to commence the divorce proceedings first will be allowed to continue with those proceedings and a second set of proceedings must be stopped or 'stayed'.

Proceedings are deemed to be commenced when one party issues or lodges them at court and takes the 'required steps' to serve the divorce papers first. Proper service is usually dependent on sending the divorce papers to 'the transmitting agency' in the relevant member state.

There are dedicated transmitting and receiving agencies in each EU member state. Broadly speaking, when divorce proceedings are commenced in one member state where another member state may also have jurisdiction, the agency in the member state where proceedings are issued, the transmitting agency, will let receiving agencies know in other relevant member states.

An obvious consequence of either or both parties to divorce proceedings having the option to issue proceedings in more than one jurisdiction is 'forum shopping'. This is simply the process of parties choosing between a number of potential jurisdictions or forums which might consider the legal application and subsequently make a decision, which is then legally binding on both parties. Choosing the best forum in any particular divorce case is likely to be an important decision to one or indeed both spouses.

Having considered which forums might accept jurisdiction, the next step is to consider what the likely  range of results might be in those different jurisdictions.  To this end, it will be important to make contact with a specialist lawyer in the applicable jurisdiction.

Obviously, in many cases it will be important to receive advice in more than one jurisdiction to establish which would be more beneficial in financial terms for the petitioning spouse. Before a foreign lawyer is instructed, it is advisable for the petitioning spouse to obtain all the necessary costs information in relation to the advice which they will receive (and how and when any payment will fall due).

Other key considerations include how difficult it might be to enforce any decision that a court in a different jurisdiction might make, and whether or not it will be convenient for either or both parties to be involved in legal proceedings in any given place. These considerations are all the more important when children are involved. Naturally, costs and language considerations will also surge to the fore.

If a particular forum in another EU member state is chosen by one party as being most beneficial to them in divorce proceedings, it is likely that it will be equally disadvantageous to the other spouse. The key issue then becomes one of securing that a particular member state will have exclusive jurisdiction and in effect be unchallengeable. This may involve a forum race to issue and take the 'required steps' for service referred to above.

It should be noted at this stage that Brussels II does not provide for spouses to decide by way of a premarital agreement which jurisdiction will deal with divorce proceedings.

In many cases, of course, it will not be necessary to think about issuing in a foreign jurisdiction or 'forum shopping'. This may be because there is no choice. However, in cases where there is a choice, the decision is often an important one.

In summary, wherever forum is an issue, there are two key action stages. First, the potential petitioner must identify any advantages or disadvantages of the forums available to him or her, from both practical and legal perspectives.

The second stage involves acting as quickly as possible to issue proceedings in the jurisdiction which the petitioner finds more attractive. In all cases, specialist legal advice should be sought as to potential jurisdictions which might be available to initiate proceedings and the potential consequences of any such action.

# Cutting the apron strings

**By Sean O'Connor    January 2005**

Let us say that you and he are buying in France together, and, as is right and proper, he is going to die first. Will you have to share the property with his children? French law is a chaotic jumble on this. I cannot sort it all out today so let us simply take a few bearings.

We need to consider three different situations:
• You are married to him, and his children are also yours. The following two solutions will normally be the best for you.

The first is *tontine,* meaning that when he dies you become the absolute owner. It is a legal freebie in the sense that the *notaire* does not charge for it. Drawbacks are that you will normally be in for some French inheritance tax when he dies, and *tontine* is not foolproof against a stroppy child if the age gap between you and your husband is more than 10 years.

Secondly, you can do something esoteric called 'change of French matrimonial regime'. You will have to get your cheque book out for the legal fees but we are not talking big bucks. When he dies you become the absolute owner just as with tontine, but you won't have to pay any French inheritance tax, and the age gap between you does not matter.

• You are married to him, but his children are born of a previous relationship. The solutions are:

(i) If he does not want to disinherit his children, he will be against the tontine clause so you can have French wills whereby he leaves a life interest in his half to you on terms that when you die, his half goes to his children. The result of this is that you can keep the property for your life time, but if you want to sell it, you must hand over some of the sale proceeds to his children.

(ii) While having French wills as above, you can also have a buy-out clause in the French deed of sale whereby you have the right to buy out his children's rights.

(iii) Alternatively, you can have the *tontine* clause, but if the age gap between you and him is more than 10 years, his children can contest the *tontine* clause in the French court.

(iv) You can change your French matrimonial regime as mentioned above, but this solution is usually not advisable in the 'previous' children

44

situation because they can contest it in the French court and have 30 years to do so from when he dies. They cannot contract out of their rights in advance.

• You and he are not married. Here the solutions are:

**(i)** Either French wills if each has previous children whose rights he wants to protect, but the wills might not be fully valid. Seek advice.

**(ii)** You can have the buy-out clause in the deed of sale whereby you can buy out his children's rights.

**(iii)** *Tontine* clause, but upon inheriting his half from him, you pay French inheritance tax on it at 60%. You can ask him to take out life cover against this. If he does not want to do so, the French wills solution will be fiscally better than *tontine* provided that the wills are in fact going to be valid. I have to omit the detail of this today.

Note that you cannot change your matrimonial regime (you are not married so you have no matrimonial regime to change).

I have omitted the use of French companies. Such a company can sometimes bring advantages, but often raises as many problems as it could solve.

It is as well to consult a lawyer on the way forward, but there may not simply be one right answer for you. Maybe you will have to weigh up the pros and cons of the options.

(The above scenarios also apply to the husband if the wife is the first to die.)

# The buying process

## By Philippe Piedon-Lavaux     February 2005

January's French Property Exhibition at Olympia attracted a great number of visitors with an interest in French properties.Having a better understanding of the process of buying in France in comparison to the UK process makes the purchase even more enjoyable. France has a system of registered titles with mostly freehold properties. The process for buying an existing house or flat in France could be divided into four different phases:

### The search and offer

Finding a property in France can be done in various ways, either with an estate agent, a French *notaire,* or directly with a seller. When visiting properties, it is essential to remember to ask about several significant issues. Points to raise should, among others, involve any recent work that has been or is being carried out at the property, any professional or building insurance in place, drainage, a list of contents, fixtures and fittings that will remain in the property, and also where the boundaries lie.

For those buying a flat in a building or a house within a housing estate, certain additional rules will apply. With regard to flats within a building (known as a building *en copropriete*), the decision-making process relating to the building and the common parts (eg common repairs or improvements) and the management bodies responsible for the running and the implementation of the decisions are largely regulated by law.

The owners of the flats within the building are collectively known as a syndicate (*Syndicat des Copropriétaires*). The syndicate is in charge of preserving and maintaining the building and administering the common parts. General meetings of the syndicate (*assemblée générale*) have the power to make decisions, subject to certain voting thresholds laid down by law being met. However, it is worth noting that each individual co-owner may have different voting rights (which will be proportional to his share of the common parts).

The actual implementation of these decisions is the responsibility of the management body know as the *Syndic* (usually an external professional management company). The rules regulating the permitted uses and restrictions on the building will be set out in the deed of conditions (*Règlement de Copropriété*) which should be provided.

Where your property forms part of an estate (as opposed to a flat within a building), the owners of the property on the estate collectively comprise an association, known as the *Association Syndicale Libre*, responsible for managing the common parts in accordance with its Articles of Association (Statuts). In addition, the *Cahier des Charges du Lotissement* (deed of conditions relating to the estate) will set out rules relating to the estate.

We would recommend making enquiries through the local *mairie* and *Direction Departementale de l'Equipement* (DDE) in relation to new developments; roads to be built or extended in the surrounding area and any planning regulations applicable to the property and its environment.

Surveys are not statutory in France and it will be up to the purchaser to appoint a surveyor at his own cost. The offer can be made verbally or in writing.

### Exchange of contract

The *compromis de vente* is the most frequently used initial contract in France for buying existing properties (excluding Paris and some places on the French Riviera where a *promesse de vente* is more often used).

This document will fix the terms of the purchase. It needs to be checked carefully. The vendor's pack, which is added to the contract, should contain the asbestos, lead and termite surveys, depending upon _where the property is located.

The agent's fees are payable by one of the parties, depending upon who will take responsibility for it.

The contract is a reciprocal binding contract by which the sellers agree to sell and the buyers agree to buy the particular property under the terms and at the price set out in the contract. This contract is usually subject to various let-out conditions (*conditions suspensives*) as most of the searches have not been carried out yet.

These are safety-net clauses, which usually cover whether or not there are any charges, outstanding mortgages, private easements, rights of way or any other private or public covenants and encumbrances on the property. A finance clause may also be included and the parties are free to agree and add other conditions (especially when the buyer needs to build or convert an existing building).

Therefore, unless a let-out condition is fulfilled or a right of pre-emption is exercised, the purchaser is not allowed to withdraw from the contract. If they do, they could lose their deposit, be compelled to execute the contract and pay the agent's fees, and be obliged to pay the seller damages.

A deposit is paid on signing the initial contract (usually 10%). After the signing of the contract the buyer will have the benefit of a seven-day cooling-off period for any second thoughts. At the end of this period the contract will be binding.

### The purchase 'structure'

Buyers should investigate the options available under both British and French law. This might include considering the structuring of the purchase through such French schemes comparable (to some extent) to a joint tenancy, a tenancy in common, a nuptial agreement, a life interest, a company or a trust.

This issue should be addressed before signing the *compromis de vente* as in some circumstances buyers may not be in a position to achieve their goals and may therefore reconsider their investment in France before finding themselves committed to the purchase.

However, it is important to remember that the appropriate structure does not generally need to be actually put in place until final completion.

### Final completion

Final completion is generally organised at the French *notaire's* office. A *notaire* does not have his equivalent in Britain. His is an independent liberal professional (ie a lawyer) to whom the state has delegated some authority. He can act for both parties. If one of the parties cannot attend the meeting, a proxy can be signed and witnessed in the UK in front of a solicitor or a public notary, as the *notarial* desk of the French General Consulates in the EU has been closed since 1 January 2005.

The balance of the purchase price plus the *notaire's* fees will need to be transferred to the *notaire's* account prior to final completion. The transfer of ownership takes place simultaneously to the transfer of the purchase price. The *notaire* will read the title to the parties or their attorney. If the parties have no comment or queries, the *notaire* will ask the parties to sign the final deed. The buyer will have to make certain the property is insured in their name from this date. Utility services will also need to be transferred into the buyer's name.

The original of the title deed will remain in the *notaire's* office. The *notaire* will then register a certified copy of the title through the French Land Registry (*Conservation des Hypotèques*). The buyer will be provided with a certified copy only (the expedition). It takes several months before receiving the title in addition to any funds held in excess from the *notaire's* fees.

# Gifting assets under French law

## By Philippe Piedon-Lavaux    March 2005

You might consider making a gift to help your relatives – or to disinherit them. From an estate planning point of view you might also make a gift in order to reduce the inheritance tax burden which will be levied on the assets to be valued on death.

When making a gift you should consider the legal aspects and French tax consequences, as these are likely to tailor the amount of assets gifted by the donor and transferred to the donee.

### Legal aspects

If a property or a share in a property in France is owned by an individual person, whether French domiciled (in the French sense of the word) or not, the registered owner is the beneficial owner of the property. If that person dies, French rules of succession will govern his French estate and the devolution of that property.

Accordingly, the rules contained in the French Civil Code which institute various compulsory rights for the benefit of the immediate family (.ie. children, and if no children then parents or/and spouse) are mandatory. They will apply to the deceased person's share in the French property, regardless of his domicile, nationality or will if drawn contrary to the compulsory rules of succession.

The compulsory rules of succession laid down by the French Civil Code require that the deceased's descendants (or parents and spouse), are entitled to a minimum portion of the estate, called the hereditary portion *(réserve héréditaire)*. The balance remaining is called the disposable portion *(quotité disponible)* and can be left by the testator to whoever he wishes.

Under the French rules of private international law, the laws of succession applying to any real estate (e.g. houses, land, flats) are the law of the place where the property is situated. The laws of succession applying to any movable assets (bank accounts, cars, contents, shares, life insurance contracts, bonds etc) will be the law of the place of domicile at the time of death, bearing in mind that France and the UK have a conflicting definition of domicile.

As the compulsory rules of succession are mandatory, any heir with protected rights may request its application in the event that the provisions of a will or a gift infringe the hereditary portion rule.

This applies to any property situated in France as well as to any movables of the deceased if the deceased was domiciled in France (from a French legal perspective) at the time of death.

Consequently if an individual wishes to exclude a person from his estate before moving to France he may try gifting some asset away, thus reducing his estate which is available for distribution. In this case the excluded beneficiary could claim from whoever benefited from the gift.

When making the gift one should consider whether the gift (*donation en advancement d'hoirie*) will be made as part of the donee's *reserve héréditaire* (if any). Then, the donor is still free to dispose of his disposable portion of his estate, which can pass under another gift, or a will. However the donor might prefer to allocate the disposable stake in his estate '*quotité disponible*' by way of a gift (*donation préciputaire*).

The freedom to dispose of your assets during your lifetime, even in the UK by way of gift, might be affected.

### Including a reservation

By transferring a property to a donee and retaining a life interest in possession, the donor will remain in the property and retain its use until his death. This will also enable him to receive any letting income from the property. The management costs and the minor repairs are usually payable by the donor.

The donee bears the responsibility for major structural repairs. On the donor's death the life interest in possession will extinguish and revert to the donee, who will be the sole owner. The tax consequences of retaining a life interest (usufruit) in the UK should be considered.

The sale of a property with such rights would require both the donor and the donee's consent.

A donor might also insist on keeping some control over the assets transferred. For example, it is possible to provide that a property which is gifted to a child has a reservation that the child should not sell it or raise money by registering a charge against it.

It is also possible to include a provision in case the donee predeceases the donor. In such an event, and also where a child divorces, the assets gifted could return to the donor.

### Gift tax

The French gift tax rates and the tax-free thresholds (i.e. the nil rate band) are generally similar to inheritance tax rates. The thresholds are based on the relationship (e.g. blood, marriage, friendship or for charitable purposes) between the donor and the donee.

Whereas a donor will be required to survive seven years in the UK, in France individuals would need to survive until the 10th anniversary of the gift to ensure that the assets gifted are excluded from the estate on death.

A major difference lies in the amount which can be transferred free of tax. In the UK one can make a gift (i.e. potential exempt transfer) free of tax if the donor survives seven years.

France is less generous. The maximum amount that can be gifted every 10 years is the tax-free threshold between the donor and the donee.

Any French based assets gifted fall under the French gift tax rules irrespective of the individual's domicile.

The gift of non-French located assets made by a non-French domiciled donor to a French domiciled donee are taxable in France, unless the donee has been domiciled in France for no more than six years of the last 10.

The French Finance Minister has indicated that he is willing to increase the number of cash transfers by parents or grandparents to the younger generation in order to bring increased spending in the high street shops.

Those moving to France might be advised to consider making gifts before becoming French tax domiciled. Obtaining tax planning advice will always remain the safest way to minimise tax, and also to plan the transfer of your assets according to your wishes.

# When is a profit not a good thing?

By Sean O'Connor    March 2005

Now that the French property market has risen in value considerably and is still rising, you may be confronted, either as vendor or purchaser, with an interesting provision of French law which in some circumstances prevents a vendor from making too much profit too soon. This is called *lesion,* literally meaning 'wound'.

If, for example, canny Mr Smith has bought cheap from Monsieur Dupont and is now selling at a huge profit to you, there are circumstances in which French law takes the view that Monsieur Dupont has been 'wounded'. He can therefore rescind his sale to Mr Smith, such that upon Smith selling to you, you don't get good title. In common parlance, Smith's sale to you is dud, because Dupont has been ripped off by Smith.

Let us examine this in more detail. Article 1674 of the French Civil Code says that if the vendor has been ripped off by more than seven-twelfths, he can rescind his sale. Article 1675 says that the property must be valued having regard to its condition at the time of the sale. So if Smith makes improvements to the property, these are taken into account. Article 1676 says that the vendor must commence his action for rescission within two years from the date of the sale. Further articles of the Civil Code say that where the case goes to court and proof of the facts is needed, the court will order three specialists to examine and report.

The way in which the calculation is done is as follows. If Dupont sold to Smith at a price, including *notaire's* fees, of 250,000 euros, and Smith is now selling to you at 450,000 euros, the difference between the two is 200,000 euros. Seven-twelfths of 450,000 euros is 262,500 euros. Since the difference of 200,000 euros is less than the seven twelfths, rip-off has not occurred.

If, however, Smith is reselling to you at 650,000 euros, the difference is 400,000 euros. Seven twelfths of 600,000 euros is 350,000 euros. Here, the difference between the two prices is more than seven-twelfths of the new price. Therefore rip-off has taken place, and Dupont can rescind, provided he brings his action within two years from the date of his sale to Smith.

You would have thought, and so did I, that the date of Dupont's sale to Smith was the date of the deed of sale. But no, it isn't. The two-year period runs from the date on which the suspensive conditions under the preceding preliminary contract of sale (*compromis de vente*) were met. This involves delving into Dupont's *compromis* with Smith and finding out when that document became legally definitive.

Assuming the figures are such that Smith has ripped Dupont off, Article 1681 of the Civil Code says that Smith can sort his problem out by paying off the amount of the rip-off less 10% of the total price. In the above example, the amount of the rip-off is 50,000 euros and when one deducts 10% of 250,000 euros plus 50,000 euros, (ie 300,000 euros) giving us 30,000 euros, you find that Smith owes 20,000 euros

If we up the ante, and Smith is now selling to you at 750,000 euros, the difference between the two prices is now 500,000 euros. Seven-twelfths of 750,000 euros is 437,500 euros. The amount of the rip-off is 62,500 euros. This plus the Dupont price of 250,000 euros comes to 312,500 euros. 10% of that is 31,250 euros. This comes off the 62,500 euros, and happens to be half of it in this example. So Smith must pay Dupont 31,250 euros to get good title. Alternatively, Smith could, if he wanted, give the property back to Dupont, and claim back the price originally paid to him.

Note that the second purchaser cannot bring the action. So all you can do is tell Smith you won't sign the deed of sale from him until Smith has sorted out his situation with Dupont.

In any case where you suspect that rip-off in this sense might have occurred, you should tell your lawyer to check the situation out. Otherwise your title will be unsound. There you are in the property having a cup of tea and along comes the postman with a court summons issued by Dupont with a view to throwing you out. Can't have that, so this is a point to be watched.

# Who can you trust?

## By Sean O'Connor    April 2005

I will start by giving a brief explanation of a trust in English law. In the late Middle Ages, from around 1300, English common law went through a period of rigidity because Parliament met so seldom. So the Lord Chancellor's court, exercising a parallel jurisdiction, imposed modifications to the common law that were by that time considered socially desirable. The Lord Chancellor was always a high-ranking ecclesiastic and his court imposed a sort of Christian conscience having regard to the needs of an evolving society. The body of case law developed by his court was and still is called 'equity'.

Suppose John has died. In his will he has left 1 High Street to his friend Richard on trust for his (John's) infant son Matthew when Matthew turns 21. In this scenario Richard, the trustee, is the legal owner of 1 High Street. So as a matter of common law he can do what he likes with it.

But equity intervenes and forces Richard to hold 1 High Street on behalf of Matthew under the terms of the trust document, or the will in this example. It is important to understand this basic concept. Richard as the trustee is the owner and Matthew, the beneficiary, is simply the person waiting for the ownership to be transferred to him when he is 21 in accordance with the trust.

Henry VIII abolished trusts by a statute of 1535 but as early as Queen Mary's reign (1553-1558) the lawyers had found a way around that statute and trusts were revived.

Thomas More was the first layman to hold the post as Lord Chancellor and it continued to be held by a layman thereafter. The Lord Chancellor's court continued to deliver judgments in matters of equity until, under the Judicature Acts of 1873-1875, the common law courts and the Lord Chancellor's court were merged into one supreme court.

In France trusts are expressly prohibited under Article 896 of the French Civil Code, except in very specific circumstances. Those circumstances are as follows: firstly, a father or mother can leave property to his or her child on terms that the child is to hand on the property to one or more of his own children (i.e. the grandchildren of the donor). Where a person does not have any children, he can leave the property to his brother or sister on terms that the donee is to hold the property on behalf of one or more children of the donee. In all other circumstances, you can't have the equivalent of a trust in France.

So how does French law treat Anglo-Saxon trusts. I will deal with this at a very simple level. Take the case of a typical British will which leaves all the testator's property to his trustees on trust for his wife if she survives him or his children if she doesn't. France will simply ignore the trust and treat the beneficiaries as the direct owners of the property to the extent that the terms of the will are in compliance with the French forced heirship rules.

However, in the case of a discretionary trust, where the trustees hold the property for the beneficiaries named by the testator as the trustees think fit, France will treat the trustees as the legal owners, which indeed under UK law they are.

This gives rise to potential fiscal pitfalls in France which have not yet, so far as I know, been tested in the French courts. For example, one trustee retires and is replaced by another, a non-relative. Is that a transfer between strangers in blood, giving rise to French gifts tax at 60%? Or again, if the trustees exercise their discretion and hand over the property to one of the beneficiaries, not a relative of theirs, is that too a transfer between strangers in blood attracting gifts tax at 60% in France? What if one of the trustees dies? Do his children compulsorily become the owners of the trust assets under the French forced heirship rules with the result that the beneficiaries of the trust lose out?

For reasons such as these, my basic advice to clients is: In France don't trust trusts. Don't go for them. Keep off them. Steer clear of them.

But it is more complicated than that. French law knows that Anglo Saxon' trusts exist. Even so, the ground is fraught with pitfalls. So if you still want to go for a trust, make sure you consult a lawyer.

# Dealing with French notaires

## By Philippe Piedon-Lavaux    May 2005

Anyone buying property in France will need to deal at some stage with a French *notaire*. This also applies for those who need to obtain mortgages, family related deeds such as nuptial agreements (marriage contracts), adoption, gifts and any transaction involving real estate such as a purchase, sale or transfer of property as part of a divorce settlement or when settling an estate.

From 2-5 May 2005 the French *notaires* will have had their Annual Congress in Nantes. The topic of the congress is 'Families without boundaries – myth or reality?'. The increase of foreign investments in France by individuals, and also marriages between foreign nationals triggers cross border tax and legal issues. We mentioned in this column last month that the European Commission is considering a new directive in relation to settling an estate with assets in several countries, for example.

*Notaires* in France are now on the front line (as are UK solicitors) when dealing with cross-border issues and the congress will help them to understand these issues better and eventually suggest some new laws to the French government.

A French *notaire* is a public official appointed by the Ministry of Justice and empowered to put the French state's seal on their deeds. These deeds fall into the category of public documents and are difficult to challenge.

These deeds are automatically evidence of their origin and of the facts and statements they record. They are also recognised as probative. The public status or authenticity of a *notarial* French act would be lost only if it is declared false judicially following a procedure known in France as 'inscription de faux'.

*Notarial* acts in addition to their probative force also enjoy executory force. Again, in order to challenge a *notarial* act and its contents, which have been checked and verified by the *notaire*, you would need to prove through a complex procedure the equivalent to the one challenging a French court order when the judge could be said not to have been impartial. The executory force of the *notarial* act enables any creditor to seek payment with a bailiff, for example, without having to obtain a court order.

There are slightly more than 7,000 *notaires*, divided all around France, who can practice either in a single practice or in partnership. It takes a minimum of seven years to become a *notaire*, and they can only start practising after they have obtained their qualification if they purchase a practice or shares in a partnership. The number of practices is closely monitored and regulated by the Ministry of Justice.

Notaires acting in their capacity as public officials in areas where they have the monopoly (e.g. conveyancing, mortgages, gifts, marriage contracts) are regulated by the Ministry of the Economy and their fees are the same all over France. For work or documents which are not subject to their monopoly fees are open to competition and agreed between the *notaire* and the clients.

*Notaires* do not prepare retainer letters when instructed unlike solicitors in the UK. Nevertheless the *notaire* has a duty of care towards his client. *Notaires* can act for several parties in the same transaction, and do not have conflict of interests as they are acting on behalf of the French State.

The *notaire* would be liable for any negligence incurred in relation to the documentation he prepares or the advice (or lack of advice) given. The concept of inadequate professional service is not as developed or regulated as in the UK. There, if a solicitor is slow and unable to organise his time in a diligent and professional manner, he might be considered as providing an inadequate professional service and liable for up to £5,000 in fines. *Notaires do* not face similar rules.

In addition, the *notaire* is insured for the work he has carried out, but there is also a professional guarantee provided by all members of this profession who are all personally liable for the work of their colleagues.

When signing documents or *notarial deeds*, a *notaire* should check the identity, the capacity and the entitlement of the individual who is signing. In addition, he should be convinced that the individual understands the legal consequences, and to what extent they will be bound by the document.

Practice shows that a number of *notaires* dealing with foreigners do not advise on all the legal consequences, and especially on cross-border issues or international tax planning matters.

It is not unusual to see a *notaire* suggesting a French solution to his UK clients which will impact badly on their position at home. This applies, for example, to people setting up French holding property companies, having a French will, or using the French usufruit, which is different from a life interest.

Your redress for bad advice or professional misconduct should first be dealt with by the head of the departmental local chamber of *notaires,* the authority responsible for all complaints. If things do not seem to move we would recommend registering the complaint with the prosecutor's office and contact a French litigation lawyer i.e. an *avocat.*

# Going nowhere slowly

**By Sean O'Connor    May 2005**

What is your legal position if your tenant won't get out of your property or you have been saddled with a squatter which, I regret to say, has become a French word?

First, if the tenancy is unfurnished it must normally be for a minimum period of three years, renewable for successive periods of three years unless, more than six months prior to the expiry of each three-yearly period, you give the tenant notice to quit, doing so by recorded delivery letter with advice of delivery. Your notice must either state you have decided to reoccupy the property or to sell it, or state some lawful and material reason for non renewal, such as any failure by the tenant to comply with his obligations.

Instead of six months' notice, you can give one month's notice if you have lost your job or have found a new job upon losing your old one.

If you have a precise professional or family reason for needing an agreement running for a period shorter than three years, the agreement must specify the reason and in those circumstances the minimum period is one year.

The agreement must be in writing and must state certain specified particulars. Therefore there is no danger of creating it by accident as it were, but you will see from the above that you will only put an end to it by carefully following the prescribed procedure.

In the case of a furnished letting, none of the above rules apply. Thus a furnished letting agreement automatically expires on its stated expiry date. It can be a spoken agreement, although it is unwise to have nothing in writing. There is no prescribed minimum time. Thus a furnished holiday let of a cottage for one week is perfectly legal.

Whatever the type of tenancy, unfurnished or furnished, if the tenant refuses to get out or if you have a squatter, the position is as follows: you cannot kick him out using force. You must obtain a court decision and serve a court order to quit on the tenant. The tenant has a minimum of two months from when the court order is served on him to move out. In winter the court will grant an extension of time not exceeding three months. Notwithstanding what has just been said, the court can grant further time, from three months to a maximum of three years, where it is necessary to rehouse the person who has been ordered to quit, and this applies just as much to squatters as to ex-tenants.

Normally there will be an initial court order subject to, in effect, a rehousing report, that is to say an enquiry as to whether the tenant or squatter is to be rehoused, and if not where he is going and whether the final order to quit is appropriate.

These enquiries are carried out by the Directorate for Sanitary and Social Affairs *(Direction de Affaires Sanitaires et Sociales or* DASS for short). Only after the report is made is the final and binding order to quit granted.

As you have seen from the, story on page 60 of this issue, in the case of a devious squatter who knows his rights and plays the system, it might, in extreme circumstances, take you three to years and five months to get rid of him.

However, when the Order for Enforcement is eventually issued it says the French Republic orders all bailiffs to implement and all commanders and officers of the public force to *'preter main-forte'* upon legally being called upon to do so, in other words grab the recalcitrant ex-tenant or squatter and bundle him out.

Patience is a virtue. Meanwhile, I would take up those references if I were you.

# Property use rights

By Philippe Piedon-Lavaux    June 2005

As we move into summer some of our readers may be thinking of looking for a cottage in the French countryside. Issues they may come across include buying land which is or could be used for farming, and the employment of people to look after the house in their absence.

It is not unusual to find that a neighbour or local farmer uses your meadows for growing hay or grazing his cattle. This is an issue which should not be overlooked, as it is not the vendor who is maintaining the land, but rather a third party who has often done this for some time. You may be informed that there is no written agreement and it is based on a 'gentleman's agreement'.

For example, you might be told that the neighbour or local farmer uses your land and in return he maintains the land and performs other services such as deterring trespassers and looking after your property.

This should not deter you from purchasing a property with land, but you should be aware that statutory farming regulations apply to farming leases when the following three conditions are fulfilled:

**1)** You receive a consideration for letting somebody else use the land (i.e. you receive something, in the form of money or services in exchange of the use of the land).

**2)** The rented land is large enough to sustain agricultural use.

**3)** The rented land is used for an agricultural or farming purpose.

It is important to realise that under the French Farming Act 1946, should you and the neighbour or farmer fulfil the conditions there will be an implied minimum nine-year lease.

Anyone who wants to sell excess grass from his land or allow cattle to graze there might therefore fall under the Farming Lease Act 1946. We would recommend you ensure that this sale or use does not occur repeatedly with the same neighbour or farmer. It is also advisable to ensure he does not contribute by any means to the property or land maintenance or provide any services or food in exchange.

Otherwise the farmer is entitled to a pre-emption right, which gives him the right to buy the property above any other purchaser should you wish to sell. (This does not apply to gifts, or when the property passes through an estate or is transferred into a company's name.)

There is also an automatic right of renewal, although the owner can override this under strict conditions, such as recovering the land for farming it himself. Furthermore, should the tenant die the lease will pass to his surviving spouse and/or children if they are in a position to continue farming on it.

If the farmer does not pay any rent he might perform services instead. French courts have ruled on several occasions that maintenance works and/or deliveries of crops or food amounted to rent in kind. It may appear that a one-off agreement is less dangerous, but as soon as the agreement is renewed it should automatically qualify as a farming lease.

Although the law does not apply to the maintenance of land immediately surrounding a house used as a dwelling, an individual buying a countryside property should be wary of the current and/or intended use of the land.

In addition, some purchasers may let a family or individual stay at the property as house-sitters. In most cases they stay without any written agreement, and the owner allows them to use the house as their main home without paying any rent. However, they will be required to help you when you use the property and may also carry out some maintenance and gardening works.

France has statutory Lease Acts, which regulate the rental of furnished or unfurnished properties. However, these do not apply when there isn't any rent payable, rather a rent in kind by performing maintenance services etc. The right to use the property would in that case constitute a salary instead (which is subject to labour law).

You should therefore take legal advice when lodging people in your home.

# Time to reflect

**By Sean O'Connor    June 2005**

The French weekly magazine *Le Point* dated 19 May 2005 ran an article headed 'The Dream of a Green Paradise', all about country cottages in France. It quotes Monsieur Hervé Blairey, the chairman of the large, all-over-the-place French Estate Agency Century 21, as saying: "All the French who have the means are tempted to purchase a country cottage. Among the purchasers of second homes, 20% are workers, 22% are white collar employees, and 27% are senior executives. The workers invest on average 86,000 euros and the executives 185,000 euros".

The article also says there are about 2.4 million second homes in France, of which 240,000, i.e. 10%, are owned by foreigners. We also get told that in many areas of France it is the Parisians or other large city dwellers that are bumping prices up, not the foreigners. Generally, prices went up 6% last year. Since then, the article says, the increase has slowed down. Hervé Blairey is quoted as saying: "I don't think we have reached the ceiling". It seems the market is stabilising somewhat, but still edging up.

In this situation and faced with the estate agent's blandishments, can you safely sign an offer to purchase document (*compromis de vente*), and do you have any rights to back out?

Firstly, please carefully note that if you are buying a building plot you do not have a right to cancel. Again, the right to cancel does not apply if you are purchasing business premises. The right only applies to residential premises. Moreover the right only applies to individual purchasers. So if you are signing as a director of a company the right does not apply. The law requires that you be handed or sent a notice giving you seven days within which to cancel, together with a copy of the contract signed by the vendors as well as by you. If, as often happens, the estate agent hands you the notice together with a copy of the contract bearing your signature but not the vendor's, the notice is not validly served.

The notice is often served in the form of an acknowledgment of receipt of it, which you have to sign. Such texts usually bear the French word 'récépissé' at or near the top. 'Récépissé' is a bureaucratic word meaning a receipt of a document. Sometimes you now get an abbreviated English translation of the notice, but usually the notice is still being sent out in totally gobblygooky French. It will contain references to Article L 271-1 of the Code of

Construction and of Habitation and Article L 271-2 of the said code.

If the notice is validly served on you, the seven days run from the day next following the date on which the notice was handed to you or (if sent by post) the day after the date on which you receive it. If you want to exercise your right to cancel, you must do so within the seven days by letter by recorded delivery with advice of delivery or by any other means presenting an equivalent certainty of delivery. It seems, though this is not clear, that emails and faxes are not sufficient and that you should also send the necessary letter by post.

You don't have to sign the receipt of notice document in the estate agent's office if you want the contract vetted by a lawyer. Lawyers inevitably juggle with several files at once, so cannot guarantee to turn the work round within the seven days in every case. When you have had time to think and your lawyer has given his okay, then you can let the notice be served. Theoretically the time between signing the contract and the receipt of notice is unlimited, but few French agents will tolerate much more than a week or 10 days wait.

# The importance of location

By Sean O'Connor    July 2005

Let's suppose that you have £100,000 sitting in a bank account in England. Do you think it's your money? No, it's not! It is a debt owed by the bank to you.

So if you die domiciled in France, can that greedy Chancellor of the Exchequer hit your hundred grand with UK inheritance tax? No he cannot! For under the double tax treaty, debts are deemed to be situated at the place where the deceased person was domiciled at the time of his death, meaning France in your case.

Now there you are living in France, and a cheque for the proceeds of sale of a house you have recently sold in the UK is sitting in your solicitor's out tray in England at the very time when you pop your clogs. Is the cheque, topping a good £400,000, located in England and can the Chancellor tax it? No! The cheque is deemed to be situated in France.

At the time when you died, you also owned £250,000 of UK government bonds. Surely they must be located in the UK and the Chancellor can therefore hit them with his cricket bat, says you. No they're not and no he cannot! They are deemed to be in France. The Chancellor is left seething with rage on the White Cliffs of Dover.

Just before you died, you took out a UK patent for a marvellous new machine to make cigarettes smell like lavender. Very valuable patent just now, you appreciate. Is the patent and its value located in the UK? Non, non et non. Under the double tax treaty it is deemed to be located in France.

Just before you died, an endowment policy issued in the UK matured in the sum of another £150,000 (I must say you are emerging as quite wealthy). Are the monies payable under the policy located in the UK and is the Chancellor a sort of croupier about to sweep 40% of them in? Answer no! The policy monies are deemed to be located in France.

At the time of your death you held roughly another £500,000 in shares quoted on the London Stock Exchange in companies incorporated in the UK. Where were they located at the time of your death? By now, you think I am going to say France, don't you? Well I have to say that here the Chancellor's luck has turned. The shares in companies incorporated in the UK are deemed under the double tax treaty to be located in the UK and so, ignoring exemptions and reliefs for present purposes, bang goes 40%, i.e. £200,000 to the Capital Taxes Office.

I am not saying that the rules under the double tax treaty for location of assets necessarily make your beneficiaries better off, because obviously the assets deemed to be located in France will be hit with French inheritance tax instead.

Even so, if you are the kind of person who likes to know which country your briefcase or handbag is located in, the rules are as interesting as they are bizarre. Anyway, you will have realised by now that when you die domiciled in France, the winding up of your estate is going to be a real wind-up.

# Winding up an estate

**By Philippe Piedon-Lavaux    July 2005**

To state the obvious, a person who dies leaves behind everything he or she owns. This property is known  as his or her 'estate'. 'Administering' an estate, describes the operations through which the property of the deceased is collected in. Any debts, legacies and taxes are paid and the legal title of ownership to the remaining property is transferred to its new owner, according to the terms of the will and the French statutory rules of inheritance.

The first point which has to be established when someone dies with assets subject to French inheritance law is whether they have left a valid will. The will must be signed in accordance with certain strict formalities laid down by statute and dealt in accordance with the French rules of inheritance, which protect children, parents, and in some cases the surviving spouse.

If a person owns a property or a share in a property in France, French rules of succession will govern his French estate and the devolution of that property. The rules contained in the French Civil Code which institute various compulsory rights for the benefit of the immediate family (.i.e children, and if no children then parents or the spouse) are mandatory and will apply to the deceased person's share in the French property, regardless of his domicile, nationality or will if drawn in contradiction to these rules.

Any heir with protected rights may request its application in the event that the provisions of a will infringe the hereditary portion rule. This applies to any property situated in France as well as all the movables of the deceased, if the deceased was domiciled in France, from a French legal perspective, at the time of death. There are usually ways to circumvent or override the impact of the French inheritance rules and anyone with a French home should seek advice in order to structure their assets in an effective way, preferably before buying the place.

**Who is liable for paying French inheritance tax?**

A tax form needs to be drawn up and lodged through the French Revenue. This fixes the taxes, which are normally payable by the beneficiaries or the legatees. It is not usually the deceased's estate (unless specified), which pays French inheritance tax but the beneficiaries of the estate, who are collectively liable for the payment of the taxes. However, general legatees are not liable for the payment of inheritance tax due by the particular legatees.

## Timescale

The time limit for lodging the tax form through the French Revenue is six months if the deceased died domiciled in France. Otherwise it is 12 months. After this deadline a fine, interest (0.75% interest per month) and penalties will be incurred.

If the deceased was French domiciled his worldwide assets will have to be declared to the French Revenue. If the deceased was non-French domiciled, only the assets located in France will have to be declared to the French Revenue, even if some of them will not be subject to any French inheritance tax (such as French bank accounts in accordance with the double tax treaty).

It is advisable to lodge a provisional tax form with a payment on account for the estimated amount of tax to pay if the deadline is missed. When lodging the tax form the payment has to be made, unless you intend claiming the benefit of a deferred payment (with a maximum of five years, chargeable interest will be due). The tax form will have to be lodged through the local French Revenue branch where the deceased person was French domiciled. If the deceased person was considered as UK domiciled the declaration will have to be lodged in Noisy Le Grand.

## Assets' value

The value of French assets is generally the value on death (eg the property market value). However, to facilitate the settlement of French estate, some of the assets can be quoted, such as the contents of properties. Specific rules apply for shares.

If the deceased was French domiciled, death will trigger an income tax statement to be lodged through the French Revenue. Income tax will be payable on any income received by the deceased from 1 January to the date of death. Death does not trigger any capital gains tax liability in France.

## Executorships

You are probably familiar with the term 'executor of a will', and may have been asked to act as one. Note that the use of executors in France is very remote and French wills do not usually contain provision with regard to executors. Their authority in France is reduced mainly because the estate is vested into the beneficiaries or legatees' names and generally not to executors. In France, the executors' role is deemed to have more moral than administrative importance.

Where some of the assets comprised in an estate are subject or governed by French inheritance law, it is important for the executors (and their advisers) to appreciate that their role is viewed very differently in France than in the UK.

### The deeds

The formalities will also include the drafting of a deed by a solicitor or a notary (i.e. *acte de notoriété*), which will indicate who is allowed to inherit and determine the beneficiaries' share in the succession according to the will (if any), the rules of inheritance and the law applicable to the estate. This will allow access to the bank accounts. Joint bank accounts should remain available to the surviving spouse, but accounts in the name of the deceased person will be frozen.

With real assets an 'attestation immobilière' should be drafted by a French notary and registered through the French Land Registry. Some have compared this document to an assent in the UK. It shows that title to the properties have passed to the deceased's beneficiaries or/and legatees. It is primarily drawn up to update the records of the French Land Registry. Dealing with an English-speaking lawyer eases the process in transferring the assets into the beneficiaries' names. The length of time and efforts involved in settling an estate in France should not be underestimated.

# French mortgages

## By Christophe Dutertre    September 2005

Over the past five years the French real estate market has increased considerably, producing concerns for investors raising finance. However, French interest rates remain low and banks still offer attractive mortgages to keep the market open for all types of investors, including first-time buyers.

British people wishing to purchase a property are eligible for a French mortgage. The procedure differs slightly from the UK, as banks operate a maximum borrowing limit from 70% to 85% of the purchase price. The bank will require a large number of documents along with the mortgage application, such as the last tax return, bank statements and an inventory of assets before they can process the application.

Once the application has been approved, an offer is issued to the purchaser who will sign and return it to the bank with a copy sent to the *notaire* who releases the funds for completion. As far as the purchaser is concerned, it will probably be the only process that he will be informed of when he purchases a property in France.

Mortgages in France are governed by the *'Lot Scrivener'* of 13 July 1979. This law is set out in articles L 312-1 and follows the Consumer Act. It sets out rules to inform and protect the borrower during an acquisition.

The procedure is usually split into three phases:

**1)** The borrower submits a loan application to several banks and discusses his project. He will usually have 15 days from signing the *compromis de vente* to submit the applications. The bank will require one or two weeks from the day it receives all the information to agree the terms and conditions of the mortgage.

At this stage it is important to ensure a clause is contained in the *compromis* enabling the purchaser to withdraw if finance cannot be obtained. If the purchaser is confident of raising the funds from another source he will have to handwrite a sentence in accordance with article L 312-16 of the Consumer Act confirming he is a cash purchaser. He will then no longer have the protection of the *Loi Scrivener*, i.e. the right to pull out of the transaction.

**2)** Once the bank has agreed the application, the purchaser receives a mortgage offer, which sets out the terms and conditions. The *Loi Scrivener* obliges the bank to maintain the terms and conditions of the mortgage for a minimum period of 30 days and gives the borrower a reflection period of a minimum 10 days before returning the signed offer to the bank. This cooling-off period was set up to protect the borrower and to ensure he fully considers the terms of the loan before committing himself. The mortgage cannot be accepted before the eleventh day and any earlier acceptance will make the offer void.

The offer will include the amount, rate, duration and a breakdown of the monthly payment. The mortgage will include personal insurance required by the bank to guarantee it is reimbursed if the borrower dies or suffers a disability. The insurance is through a national insurance company linked with the bank. It is compulsory and the bank will always refuse to pay the *notaire* if the insurance is not set up.

**3)** Finally the *notaire* will receive a signed copy of the mortgage offer and include it in the final contract. Completion can only take place at this stage. Effectively banks in France require a guarantee over the property to secure the repayment of the mortgage. The security is indicated in the mortgage offer and the *notaire* is responsible for registering it with the title deed.

Two main guarantees in the Civil Code protect the lender over the property. The most common is the *hypotheque'* (article 2114 of the Civil Code), which covers the reimbursement of any debt for the benefit of the lender. This guarantee passes on to whoever the property is sold to. It allows the bank to take the property back if the borrower fails to pay and sell at an auction. The proceeds of the auction will be transferred to the lender by preference to any other creditors (except in limited cases). The bank will ask for the *hypotheque* on your property if you wish to refinance your existing mortgage or finance renovation work.

A different guarantee is chosen when the purchase money is raised by a mortgage. This guarantee is called a *'privilege de preteur de deniers'* and is similar to a lender's lien. It provides more security for the bank than a *hypotheque*. The lender's lien is based on the idea that he contributes a particular amount to enable the purchase of a property. The money must be used only to purchase the property and the amount of the loan is protected by this lien.

The lender would normally want priority to be over all other creditors for the reimbursement of this sum. The *privilege de preteur de deniers* is a right conferred to the lender to be preferred to other creditors, even a *hypotheque*. In other words the bank will be paid first.

For this reason the bank may be reluctant to consider a further mortgage at a later stage which will only be guaranteed by a *hypotheque* and not a *privilege de preteur de deniers*.

The two guarantees to be secured on the property have to be registered through a *notaire* in France. The procedure is identical to completion of a property purchase, as the *notaire* will draw up a contract to be signed by the lender and the borrower. The mortgage deed will be registered within two months to ensure first priority for the bank. As it must be completed through a *notaire,* he will indicate to the purchaser the mortgage fees to complete the contract. The legal fees are usually indicated by the bank in the mortgage offer and should not be confused with the mortgage fees taken by the bank which are administration fees. They will represent 1-1.5% of the amount borrowed if a *privilege de preteurs de deniers* is required.

Fees for the *hypotheque* will be higher as there is a stamp duty of 0.615%.

As for reselling the property the purchaser, who will then become the vendor, may also be required to pay a *notaire's fee* to redeem the mortgage. The guarantee on the property will be effective for the duration of the mortgage plus two years. If the owner decides to put his property on the market before paying off the mortgage or before the end of the mortgage, the *notaire* has a responsibility to provide a free of mortgage property to the new owner. A deed called *'mainlevee'* will be drawn up by the *notaire* and will cancel the charge registered at the Land Registry. This contract is signed by the bank who will acknowledge the repayment of the mortgage.

# From under offer to sold

By Sean O'Connor    September 2005

Selling can be stressful. Will your buyer pay up on time? What happens if he defaults? How much money will you clear net of expenses? Here are some matters to bear in mind.

Firstly the deposit. It is wise to insist on this being 10%, as is in principle normal. The deposit has got to be enough to make the purchaser think twice about losing it, and has also got to provide you with reasonable compensation if he walks off.

Next, the purchaser's cancellation right. Unfair you might think, but when you sign the contract *(compromis de vente)* you are bound whereas when the purchaser signs it he is not. He has a seven-day cancellation right, assuming the property concerned is residential. His seven days run from when he is served with a notice. The notice must be accompanied by a copy of the contract, bearing his signature and yours.

You should lean on your agent and make sure he gets on with these formalities as quickly as possible and also that he follows the rule-book properly. If he sends out the notice with a contract that has not yet been signed by you or the purchaser, the exercise is fatally flawed and the purchaser can go on cancelling to his heart's content until the correct procedure is carried out.

Then come the suspensive conditions, particularly any mortgage that the purchaser may want and any conditions concerning outline planning permission, for example to convert a barn.

The subject-to-mortgage clause usually says that the purchaser must apply for his loan on the official form within 10 days of contract and that he must receive his offer of loan within 45 days of contract, failing which the transaction is off. The contract should state, and even if it doesn't French law provides that the purchaser must comply fully with the requirements of the lending bank, supplying all information and paperwork that the bank requires, failing which the purchaser is considered to have brought about the failure to obtain the mortgage himself. The result, in those circumstances, is that he loses his deposit.

You should also lean on your agent to make sure the purchaser actually applies for his loan within the 10 days and does, or does not, receive his offer within the 45 days. If the purchaser says his offer has been refused, you should tell your lawyer to make full enquiries as to why the application was turned down. Of course in a genuine no offer situation, you are stymied. You have waited 45 days and you have nothing to show for it. Back to square one. That's a risk you have to take. Obviously it is better to find a cash buyer if possible.

The purchaser may perfectly reasonably require a suspensive condition as to planning permission to do this or that. It is in his interest and yours that the clause is lucidly worded. It is important to make sure the application for the permission is actually lodged within, say, 10 days of contract. The planning office is supposed to reply within two months, but in many parts of France it actually does not do so for three months or even more.

So it is as well to ascertain locally how long they are taking, and to fix a completion date in consequence. It is also as well to attempt to form a view as to whether permission is likely to be granted or not. Consult your lawyer If you wait up to three months and permission is refused, you have got precisely nowhere.

French capital gains tax and UK capital gains tax are other matters to bear in mind, and seek advice on.

In France estate agent's commission is normally payable by the purchaser, but that is not always so. Therefore you should check. Unless expressly otherwise agreed, *notaire's* fees and costs are borne by the purchaser.

So to sum up, form a view of your prospective purchaser cannily. Make sure he actually wants to buy the property. There may be something to be said for pitching your price slightly on the attractive side.

# Easements and covenants

## By Philippe Piedon-Lavaux    October 2005

Anyone buying in France should naturally be concerned about rights of way, restrictions and covenants affecting a property. After all, you don't want to be disturbed or disrupted by somebody crossing your land, for example.

Various rights and obligations might apply to a property (called 'the encumbered estate') for the benefit of somebody else's property ('the dominant estate'). This could apply to maintenance and carrying out work, or could prevent the exercising of certain rights. These are known as 'easements' or 'covenants', depending on the nature of the rights or restrictions.

They might be set up to serve the interest of the public or an individual, and their origin could come from various sources. Some will arise from the natural location of a property, such as rules applying to planting trees, the distance between trees or windows and a boundary, a right of way to a property which would otherwise have no access, or a stream originating on higher land. Other easements could arise from laws or public regulations and will be statutory. A court case could also recognise an easement or covenant.

We generally distinguish between an easement, which does not require somebody's actions such as a right of view, or one which does require actions such as a right to take water from a well or a right of way. Some are apparent like a gate or window, others are not, such as a limitation to build on the land.

Water from a neighbouring property, either from the ground or from a roof, or for farming needs is likely to put a burden on owners generally. The location of buildings, trees or hedges should also be considered with regard to distance and height. It would be unfortunate not to take into account a potential claim for cutting a line of trees which has been planted too close to a boundary.

Public interest has increased the number of regulations applicable to property owners. Villages and towns expand, quality of life improves and the development of communication and transport has increased the amount of rules introduced by public authorities. These regulations might have been made in the interests of the public, which becomes an overriding interest, and not for the benefit of a particular property. For example, a property could become subject to a road-widening scheme, walls could be demolished or trees cut in order to improve road safety. It is important to remember that properties close to rivers or the sea might be subject to rights of way, and those near airports might suffer restrictions in relation to the height of buildings and pylons. Electricity lines and public drainage require access for maintenance and repair. For health and safety reasons, statutory surveys are now provided by vendors relating to asbestos, lead and termites where applicable, but hefty regulations also apply to water, wells, drainage and septic tanks.

Easements or covenants arising from public organisations should be known by the purchaser, i.e. they cannot say they were ignorant. However recent court cases have outlined a pre-contractual obligation by the vendor to inform the purchaser, but only in relation to non-apparent easements or covenants. If the vendor wants to be discharged from his duty of information he needs to disclose any restrictions which might affect the normal use of the property or those which are not foreseeable. For example, a restriction set up to protect a view over somebody else's land or a road-widening scheme would need to be disclosed by the vendor.

On the other hand French law distinguishes between easements or covenants which are public or implied from the location of the property and which should be known by the purchaser. This could apply, for example, to covenants and easements relating to airports, mines and roads. The prescription period (i.e. 30 years) is the required time for claiming the use or benefit of somebody else's property. This will apply only to apparent easements which are in continuous use such as windows overlooking a neighbouring property.

French contracts and title deeds generally include a clause indicating that the purchaser will take on the benefit or burden of any easements and covenants at his own risk. Before exchanging contracts you should carefully consider the draft contract and ensure you are sufficiently protected. It is also important to ask the professionals involved to confirm and check the previous title to the property and ask the local authorities what the position might be.

# A leap of faith

By Sean O'Connor   November 2005

December 9 2005 marks the 100th anniversary of the French law of 1905 which brought about the separation of the State from the Church. Under the French monarchy, the king derived his authority through his coronation directly from God, not the people. That idea was rejected during the turbulent years of the French Revolution, which may be said to have started with the fall of the Bastille prison in Paris on 14 July 1789. But Napoleon, with spin, continued it in an attenuated form.

On 15 July 1801, Napoleon signed a *concordat* with the Church. The preamble acknowledged the 'Catholic, Apostolic and Roman' religion as being the religion of 'the great majority of French citizens'. From then on, the French State paid the salaries of the clergy and the Church had a prominent role in national life. In the late 19th century, those who wanted a more secular society achieved political dominance, and the kw of 1905 was the result. Section 1 says that "the Republic ensures freedom of conscience". It guarantees the free exercise of religions subject to the sole restrictions laid down hereinafter in the interests of public order. Section 2 says that 'the Republic neither acknowledges any religion nor pays any salaries nor any subsidies for any religion'.

The result of all this is that since 1905 the French State has had no religion at all. It is not atheist. Its standpoint simply is that the idea of God is none of its business.

There are all sorts of practical consequences of this. For example, it is forbidden in France to put up any religious symbol or emblem on any public monuments or in any public places, except on churches, in cemeteries, on funeral monuments and in museums (section 28 of the law). Another consequence is that in France a church wedding has no legal effect at all. You must get married in the *mairie* (town hall).

The separation between Church and State is, however, less rigorous than originally intended. This brings me to an interesting aspect, indeed quirk, of French properly rights. By a compromise implemented in 1907 and thereafter, the State is the owner of the then existing church buildings but makes them available to the Church. Thus when you see an old village church in France, if you think that the Catholic Church owns it, you are wrong. If you think you can come along and buy it, you are wrong again.

The local commune, meaning the municipality, is the legal owner of it, but, by law, must make it available to the Church and must maintain and repair it.

Another attenuation of the principle of separation is that nowadays the State provides subsidies to church schools. That is still a somewhat divisive matter in France. Atheism has had a good run and although it is probably somewhat on the wane, there are still, particularly among the older generation, a significant number of people who do not want the State to have anything at all to do with the Church.

How is religion getting on in France now? Behind a deceptive facade of consumerist secularism, better than you might think. In March 2003, a poll was carried out concerning the French and their beliefs, and the results were Roman Catholics 62% of the population, Muslims 6%, Protestants 2%, Jews 1% and no religion at all 26%.

Catholics represent almost two-thirds of the population so in that sense France can still be described as a Catholic country, but it is important to understand that the French State is certainly not Catholic. That has been the situation for 100 years now. So far so good, or bad, whichever way you look at it.

Can France, or come to that can we, get on without God for another 100 years? I do not think so, but that, of course, is a speculation and another matter entirely.

# Selling a French property

**By Philippe Piedon-Lavaux    November 2005**

Selling a property should be a straightforward process - -put it on the market through an estate agent, find a buyer, agree a price and wait for the sale to proceed to completion. However, it is not as simple as it appears and vendors might be surprised by all the documents, formalities and information they will have to provide, and it is also likely to trigger tax implications.

### Estate agents/notaires

The easiest way to market your property is to advertise it through an estate agent. They will ask you to sign a mandate to market the property and agree a fee for their work. Estate agent's fees are not regulated and are generally calculated on the property's value. Should you use a *notaire,* his commission and fees are regulated and should not exceed 5% plus VAT up to 45,735 euros and 2.5% plus VAT above. The vendor will have to agree a net price.

You have the option to sign an exclusive mandate, specifying that you are not allowed to advertise the property through another agent for a fixed period, or a normal mandate, which provides flexibility to market it elsewhere.

### Price

There are some legal aspects to a sale that vendors must consider, if the sale price exceeds seven-twelfths of the initial purchase price and if the sale takes place within two years. The vendor could be hit with a claim from his previous vendor for loss and unfair advantage - when selling a property for 120,000 euros the vendor should ensure he did not purchase it for less than 50,000.

### Capital gains tax/VAT

The resale of the property usually attracts capital gains tax unless you can claim exemption. The rate applicable for non-French residents residing in the EU is 16%. A tapering relief of 10% will apply after the fifth year, in addition to an allowance of 1,000 euros. Above 150,000 euros the vendor will have to appoint a tax representative at their cost.

A recent instruction dated 4 August 2005 ruled that renovation work on the property can only be deducted in specific cases and only if they were carried out by a builder. Personal work and materials purchased by the owner no longer reduce the gain. Reconstruction work, the creation of additional living areas, and renewal of facilities, such as rewiring to bring it up to standard, are the only works that can be taken into consideration. After five years the vendor can claim a 15% allowance without proving any works done.

The resale of a newly-built property less than five years old will attract VAT on the sale price. VAT will only apply on the first resale and then stamp duty is payable for the following transactions. VAT may also be due for new living areas in the property or a renovated barn. It is the vendor's responsibility to declare if the property is subject to VAT. In that case the price will be split between VAT payable by the vendor on the new part and stamp duty on the old part. The vendor can offset the VAT paid on the original purchase price or works that have been carried out.

## Charges

French banks usually make a charge to guarantee the loan. If the vendor has not redeemed the loan by the time of sale, the *notaire* will pay it off from the proceeds - he will confirm the charge has been removed and the property is free of any loan. The charge will last for the duration of the initial mortgage, plus two years. Therefore, even if the vendor paid off the mortgage before its end and then sold the property, the formality is still required at his cost.

## 10-year guarantee/insurance

A purchaser buying a new property, or one subject to major renovation or refurbishment, will require the 10-year guarantee, the French NHBC, contracted by the builder who carried out the works. This insurance is compulsory for professionals such as developers when they sell properties off-plan. If a vendor fails to hand over the documents, they will remain liable to the purchaser for any damage that should have been covered by the guarantee. If builders carried out the work, the vendor should be able to chase them for it, providing they are also covered by insurance, if not he will have to prove their negligence.

## Compulsory surveys

Vendors have to produce an information pack, including an asbestos survey, if the property was built before 1 July 1997, and termites and lead poisoning surveys depending where the property is situated. A decree dated 8 June 2005 is due to come into force ruling that the vendor will have to supply surveys on asbestos, termites, lead poisoning, gas system, drainage, technological and natural risks. This new document is an important step towards informing and protecting the purchaser.

**Letting**

With a leased property, whether it be farming land or a dwelling, the tenant may be entitled to a pre-emption right. The vendor would have to inform the *notaire* and the purchaser of any lease, verbal or written, applicable to ensure vacant possession. For instance, giving a farmer access to a field for his cattle in return for him looking after a property may constitute a farming lease.

**Condominium block**

Vendors have to settle any outstanding management fees prior to the sale. The *notaire* may have to wait until he receives clearance from the managing agent that the vendor has paid his charges before releasing funds.

# The civil code

**By Sean O'Connor    January 2006**

Napoleon, towards the end of his life, took the view that the Civil Code was the most significant of his achievements. He said: "My true glory does not consist of having won 40 battles. Waterloo will wipe out the memory of so many victories. But nothing will wipe out my Civil Code. It will live for ever."

Before the French Revolution, which started in 1789, different laws applied in different parts of France. In the south Roman law prevailed. In the north laws going back to the time of the Franks, Burgundians and Visigoths dominated. Such inconsistency was totally incompatible with the revolutionary ideal of one unified French State. Between 1789 and 1799, several preliminary attempts were made to draw up a Civil Code.

Napoleon came to power in a coup d'état which took place on 10 November 1799. On 12 August 1800 he appointed a commission consisting of four lawyers representing different regions of France, to finalise the text. Napoleon attended in person 36 of the commission's 87 meetings. The Code reproduced many of the provisions of pre-revolutionary law (*l'ancien droit*). It also included the essential of the thousands of enactments churned out during the revolutionary period. The draft text was completed by the end of 1801 but the Code was not promulgated until 21 March 1804. Henceforward France was to have one set of laws for the whole country.

Civil law covers all matrimonial and family matters, including wills and inheritance, parental authority, and legal capacity. It also covers all property rights, mortgages, contracts, guarantees, and wrongs such as negligence. You can see from all this that the drawing up of the Code constituted a massive undertaking.

The Civil Code represents a mix of liberalism and conservatism. Most of the gains made during the revolutionary period, and in particular the equality of all citizens before the law, freedom of religion, and the abolition of feudalism were retained. Property rights, which had been disputed during the Revolution, were asserted. The Code also strengthened the legal position of men in relation to women by making the husband the ruler of the household. So under the Civil Code the legal status of women was lower than it had been prior to the Revolution. This was in line with Napoleon's attitude to his wife Josephine whom he divorced, Henry VIII style, telling her brutally "I need a womb" when she failed to bear him an heir.

That, of course, has now changed. Since 1804 there have been innumerable amendments to the Civil Code to bring it into line with present day social realities. However, one of the original articles that has never been changed, and is of particular interest to French property owners, is Article 3, which says: 'Real properties, even those possessed by foreigners, shall be governed by French law'. Napoleon may have lost Trafalgar and Waterloo but your French property is still, so to speak, under his cannon. *Fraternité?* That's not in the Code, so don't go there!

# Civil partnerships

## By Christophe Dutertre    January 2006

The Family Proceeding Rules 1994 have recently been amended with the introduction of a Civil Partnership Act 2004 that came into force on 5 December 2005. This act will enable same sex couples to register a partnership, which will have identical rules to marriage. France has already adopted the same concept for unmarried couples with the 'pacte civil de solidarité' (PACS), introduced 15 November 2005. The rules of the PACS are regulated by articles 515-1 and follow the Civil Code.

The PACS, contrary to the Civil Partnership Act 2004, is a contract made by two adults of the same or opposite sex to organise their lives. Like the Civil Partnership Act 2004, it sets out the rights and duties of partners and requires formalities regarding the registration and termination.

### Conditions for a PACS

The PACS is only permitted for unmarried individuals who have not already contracted a PACS with a third party. It will be prohibited within degrees of relationship. For instance, adopted children, siblings and step-parents with children cannot contract a PACS. As the PACS is a contract the rules regarding consent will also be applicable.

The law obliges partners who declare a PACS to provide the civil court with two original copies of the written contract. No particular form is required and the partners could prepare the contract themselves or request the assistance of a lawyer (*avocat* or *notaire)* to guide them. The authentic form required for a transaction such as a purchase or gift of real estate is not required and the *notaire* would only ask the partners to sign an undersigned agreement (*acte sous seing privé).*

### Registration of the PACS

The PACS has to be registered at the civil court (*greffe du tribunal de grande instance* for non residents). Two people who wish to enter into a PACS should make a joint declaration at the civil court. They register the contract at the court, and add documents showing their civil status which establishes the validity of the transaction with respect to Article 515-2, together with certificates showing their places of birth.

Once they have complied with the above rules the court enters the declaration into a registered book. Should the partners decide to amend their

PACS they would have to lodge this with the court office that received the initial transaction.

**Effects of the PACS**

The effect and consequences of the PACS depends on your residency. Some rules will only apply if you are French residents, others such as French assets and tax consequences concern both UK and French residents.

For those who elect residency in France, the PACS sets out the obligation of mutual assistance that is compulsory during the PACS. Any clause that restrains this obligation would be invalid. However, unlike marriage, the PACS would not create any obligations for the partners to live together or to be monogamous.

The partners will be obliged to financially assist each other in day-to-day life. They will be responsible for the partner's debts linked to the maintenance of the common home, i.e. local taxes, insurance and rent. Mortgages taken out by one partner will not oblige the other to its reimbursement.

In terms of income tax the PACS will also allow you to lodge a joint tax form and benefit from the advantages of a married couple. As far as assets are concerned, again the difference will depend on your residency. If you are resident in France, all moveable assets bought during the PACS are deemed jointly owned (unless there is a specific clause setting out their ownership). Partners have the freedom to insert a clause in the PACS contract dealing with their future assets.

Immoveable assets follow the same rules for non-residents and residents of France, if the partner who purchases them does not indicate in the final contract his intention that the property remain in his estate. The co-ownership rules will apply regarding the administration and disposition of it.

**Inheritance tax**

One of the attractions of the PACS is the tax allowances. Partners owning a property in France are taxed at a high rate of 60% on the share inherited after benefiting from a threshold of 1,500 euros. Partners who enter into a PACS will be able to benefit from a threshold of 57,000 euros before being taxed at a rate of 40% up to 15,000 euros and 50% above. The tax remains high but can simplify the transfer of a property to the partner without being obliged to sell the real asset to pay them.

**Termination of the PACS**

In accordance with Article 515-7 of the Civil Code the PACS will terminate in the following cases:

**1)** Partners decide by a mutual agreement to put an end to a PACS. In that case they must file a joint written declaration with the civil court.

**2)** If one of the partners decides to put an end to a PACS, he or she will serve notice of his or her decision and send a copy of that notice to the civil court.

**3)** If one of the partners puts an end to a PACS by marrying, they should notify their decision by recorded letter to the other partner, and should send copies of the letter and of his/her record of birth on which mention of the marriage has been made, to the Civil Court.

**4)** A PACS would come to an end if one of the partners dies.

# So you think you're French...

**By Philippe Piedon-Lavaux    February 2006**

It will be no surprise to learn that with the wave of couples relocating to France becoming younger and younger, reported cases are starting to trickle through regarding divorces.

Despite the better weather and lifestyle, the stresses and strains of starting again in another country, maybe worsened by financial worries, can tip an unhappy marriage into a broken one.

For many of those who decide to move to France it is with the intention to live there permanently, but they should be aware that if the marriage breaks down divorce proceedings could  be issued in either the UK or France. Under the Brussels II Treaty of 29 May 2000 if both spouses are habitually resident in France, or the applicant is habitually resident there for at least a year immediately before the  issue of the petition, the French courts can be used, for example.

The spouses would need to take advice about the choices open to them according to their circumstances. If they had a choice as to where to institute proceedings, they would need to take advice from lawyers well versed in dealings in the relevant jurisdictions as to which would be most beneficial to them. Obviously, the way in which French jurisdiction would treat a pre-nuptial or post-nuptial agreement could be a key consideration.

Such nuptial agreements are not binding in the courts of England and Wales. If the divorce proceedings are initiated in these courts, they will have discretion as to how the matrimonial assets are distributed, including those situated in France, and will apply British law. The impact of a nuptial (or post-nuptial) agreement will not be substantial, particularly where there are children.

Therefore, when considering divorce proceedings in England, a decision has to be made regarding domicile.

This was the very issue decided in a recent case named RvR 2006. The couple were married for more than 20 years and had eight children, seven of whom were born in England. However, before the birth of the youngest child the family decided to move to France where they already owned two properties. Their English home was sold together with two English investment properties, and the family lived in France for nine years until the marriage broke down.

To all intents and purposes, the family lived 'a French life', with the children attending French schools. However, the husband filed for divorce in England on the basis that both parties were domiciled in England. In her original acknowledgment of service (the reply that the respondent gives to the divorce petition), the wife gave France as her country of habitual residence and England as her country of domicile and nationality. She subsequently asserted France as her domicile. She tried to stop the English divorce petition proceeding. However, she was not successful and the court said that it would be difficult to persuade them that by merely living in France she had stopped being English for the purposes of the divorce proceedings.

The facts that worked against the wife were that she could not demonstrate a real connection with France or integration into French life. She did not vote or obtain a *carte de séjour.* Instead, she kept many of her connections with England, such as her driving licence, passport, sole nationality, bank accounts, credit cards and private medical cover. In addition, the family were supported by income earned in England.

This must be the position facing many families who would find it difficult to show that they had a fixed and settled intention to abandon an English domicile of origin and make a new home in France for an indefinite time.

It is important to get specialist advice in this complicated area of law, particularly where there is a choice of jurisdiction as one party might do better under the English system of divorce rather than the French system – and speed is of the essence.

# Winding up an estate

By Sean O'Connor    February 2006

Your husband has died. He has left a will appointing you as his executor and leaving everything to you.

There are two children born of your marriage to him, no others. His estate consists of a house in France and a large portfolio of shares, worth one million pounds in UK companies, handled by a portfolio manager in London.

In which country was your husband domiciled at the time of his death? Well in your case, you and he quit England five years ago. He had sold the house in Islington, which was in his own name. This explains why the million-pound portfolio is also in his name only. The house in France was bought with some of the proceeds of the sale. It, too, is in his name. You and he had had enough of England, all those speed cameras, and had gone to live in France permanently and for ever. So your husband died domiciled in France.

Do you get the French property under his will? The answer to this is that you get one third and the two children take one third each, because that is the compulsory entitlement of the children under French law. Nevertheless, since the residence is your principal residence, you have an exclusive right to live in it for the rest of your life.

Does the portfolio go to you under your husband's will? French law and British law are agreed in saying that moveables devolve in accordance with domicile. As has been ascertained above, your husband died domiciled in France. So French law applies to the devolution of the UK portfolio. Therefore your two children each get one third of it, and you only get the remaining third.

Does French inheritance tax have to be paid on the French house? Yes. You get 76,000 euros free of tax, and the two children each get 50,000 euros free of tax. The family gets another 50,000 euros free of tax. Then the tax must be paid at approximately 20%.

Does the UK portfolio get hit with French inheritance tax? In principle the answer is yes but the inheritance tax paid in the UK is deductible from the French inheritance tax bill. Since UK inheritance tax is 40%, French inheritance tax will only apply to the one third of the portfolio you inherit (because there is no inheritance tax between husband and wife in the UK) and to the nil rate band for the purposes of UK inheritance tax, currently £275,000.

Does the UK portfolio get hit with UK inheritance tax? As already explained, not on your one third nor, above that amount, on the nil rate band of £275,000. Above that though the answer is yes, notwithstanding the fact that your husband left everything to you in his will.

Can you and the children directly tell the portfolio manager to hand over the assets? No. You must first get probate of the will. This means that the UK court confirms the validity of the will and confirms the vesting of the assets of the deceased in the executrix, namely yourself.

How long does this process take? This scene is administratively complicated, so you are looking at several months in practice. You first of all have to pay the UK inheritance tax. Can you use the million pounds to pay it? No. You must either borrow against the portfolio or pay the UK inheritance tax out of your own pocket. Then you apply for probate.

What happens when probate has been obtained? You can then tell the portfolio manager to sell the shares and send the million pounds to you. After that, you are under a legal duty to pay each of the children their one-third share minus the inheritance tax you have paid on their share. You will also deduct from their share any French inheritance tax that has to be paid and is attributable to them. You also have to pay your own French inheritance tax bill.

The remainder of the kitty will be yours to rebuild your life with.

# The false lease affair

## By Sean O'Connor    March 2006

Truth is stranger than fiction. Although I have altered this case a little, it is based on a matter that I handled over a number of years.

My client was driving to the farm in France that he had recently bought with his wife in joint ownership. He had invested his life savings in it, and it was to be their retirement home, where they were going to carry on a small-scale farming operation for their bread and butter.

When he arrived, he wasn't allowed in. He was informed he had signed a nine-year continuously renewable lease in favour of his son and his wife at a derisory rent. The local gendarmes were called in. They arrived flexing their muscles and stomping their boots, and ordered my client to leave. He soon discovered that his signature had been forged by his wife on a bogus lease. The next thing he learned was his wife had run off to Portugal with another man.

After a while, he was involved in two different legal actions before the local French court, one to strike out the bogus lease and kick out his son and daughter-in-law from the property, the other to divide up the farm between him and his by now ex-wife.

Astonishingly, and as if his life wasn't bad enough, he lost the repossession action at first instance. The regional court based its decision on Article 1427 of the French Civil Code which, somewhat freely translated, says: 'If one of the spouses has exceeded his or her powers over the jointly owned property, the other spouse can apply for the cancellation of the act concerned. The action for cancellation is available to the other spouse for two years from the date on which he became aware of the act.'

The court ruled that as more than two years had gone by from the time when my client became aware of the forged lease until he commenced his action, he was out of time. Bang had gone his life savings, or so it seemed.

Fortunately, he had instructed a solicitor back home in the UK. I noticed that Article 1427 of the Civil Code came within a portion of the Code that governs relations between husband and wife when they are married under the matrimonial regime implied by French law. But my client was married in England, under English law, so Article 1427 did not apply to him and his wife. Nor did the two-year deadline for bringing an action. In fact, he had 30 years within which to bring his action for dispossession from when he was refused access to the property. So he went to the Court of Appeal.

The court ruled that I was perfectly right. Moreover it pointed out that Article L. 411-4 of the Rural Code says that contracts for rural leases must be in writing. The bogus lease was not 'in writing' because my client hadn't signed it. So there was no lease. Accordingly, the court ordered his son and wife to quit, granting repossession to my client and his ex-wife.

The ex-wife, who was by then short of a bob or two, and who was entitled to a one-half interest, wanted to sell it for a song. My client refused. In the end, he found a purchaser at a very good price. He extracted a power of attorney for sale out of his ex-wife. Property values had risen meanwhile so in the end he got most of his money back. There is an amiable French expression 'bonne continuation'. It means 'have a good life from now on'. And so he did.

# Lettings and leases

**By Matthieu Prevost   March 2006**

Buying a small place in France to rent can be a good source of income. A leaseback might be an appropriate investment for those keen on a long-term renting agreement, while others may prefer to rent the property themselves rather than via a letting company.

Seasonal lettings for short stays are set out by the provisions of the French Civil Code. However, these rules must be supplemented by some extra requirements when the rented accommodation falls under specific legislation such as 'meublé de tourisme', Gîtes de France, or when the landlord is deemed to be professional by the number of dwellings rented out

Seasonal renting (*location saisonnière*) is a form of lease in France for occupying a property for a short period of time (e.g. one week, several weeks, a few months). Seasonal renting overcomes the rules set out by the Residential Property Act dated 6 July 1989 and modified in 1993. The booking of a *location saisonnière* is often agreed over the phone or via a brochure or the internet where the need to send a detailed and exact description is essential. Should the description be inaccurate, this could trigger a fine and/or cancellation of the lease by the tenant due to misrepresentation on the part of the landlord.

After receiving the description of the accommodation, the tenant's agreement can be confirmed by sending a deposit to the landlord or his representative. Should the landlord wish the deposit to be used as a penalty if the tenant cancels, then this must be stipulated in writing.

The lease must include some essential clauses. These relate to the length of the stay (case law has considered that seasonal renting should generally not exceed six months); the amount of rent; running costs, ( if not included in the rent), and the terms and conditions of the lease. Additional clauses can be added, such as the exact number of tenants, having pets in the property or the obligation to subscribe to civil liability insurance.

Once the lease is agreed, both parties are bound. The tenant will have to respect the lease and the landlord must allow the tenant to occupy the dwelling peacefully. The landlord should do nothing to restrict the use of the rented property unless it was outlined in their agreement. This obligation relates not only to the property but also to all the ancillary facilities. The tenant can ask for damages or even cancellation of the lease if the landlord carries out work, which makes the property (or part of it) uninhabitable.

The second set of regulations results mainly from the Residential Tenancy Act dated 6 July 1989, applicable to long-term leases for unfurnished properties. If you wish to invest in France and intend to rent unfurnished, this is the contract you will probably be signing with your tenant. The rules set out by this act are usually similar to the common law regarding the landlord's and tenant's obligations (for example delivering the property in a good state by the landlord, paying the rent in due course by the tenant).

A written document is required, setting out names, addresses and description of the property, as well as the general conditions of the lease. The contract is automatically signed by the parties for a minimum period of three years for an individual and six years when the tenant is a company. As the rules are *d'ordre public* it is not possible to change them and agree a shorter term unless the landlord can give a valid reason provided by the Residential Tenancy Act.

The main characteristic of the lease is to provide the tenant with secure accommodation. The tenant is entitled to automatic lease renewal at the expiry date for another three (or six) years and a landlord will only be able to terminate the lease in three cases:

• If he wishes to claim the property for his or his family's personal use.

• If he decides to sell, in which case he must offer it to the tenant who has a first right of refusal.

• If the tenant fails to pay the rent. However, a very exacting procedure must be triggered before the tenant can be evicted.

A guarantor might be named in the contract to secure the payment of rent in the event the tenant fails to pay.

It is a good idea to seek advice before formalising such a document as it could help to assess the conditions and consequences. The signing of a lease drafted with your lawyer will always give you more protection if you are the landlord rather than a simple document signed with an independent agent.

# That's VAT

**By Sean O'Connor    May 2006**

Naturally enough, since most things in French are the other way round, value added tax, i.e. VAT, is *taxe sur la valeur ajoutée,* or TVA for short. The normal rate of VAT in France is 19.6% although in certain circumstances the so-called reduced rate of 5.5% is charged.

VAT at 19.6% is chargeable on new buildings. The charge applies on the first sale of a new building within five years from the completion of the construction works. This is the date on which the *déclaration d'achèvement* (declaration of completion) is lodged at the local town hall (*mairie*). If you buy a new-build property from a developer, the charge is included in the price you pay. If you sell it on within five years from the date of the completion of the construction works, your purchaser doesn't pay VAT because you have already paid it.

If you buy a plot of land and build a house on it, and then sell it within five years from the completion of the construction works, your buyer pays the VAT, and you account for it to the French tax administration because your sale constitutes the first sale within the five-year period. If you wait six years from the completion of the construction works and then sell, your purchaser does not pay VAT and you do not have to account to the tax administration for VAT.

If you buy an apartment in an officially approved *residence de tourisme* on leaseback terms, you don't pay the VAT, provided that the total leaseback period is 20 years. If you sell within this period, you must pay back a proportion of the VAT. There is a legal flaw in such leaseback schemes because under French law the lessee has a right to renew for ever, meaning you take an initial risk of never getting your property back. Take legal and commercial advice before signing up to any such deal.

I have had a few developer clients wanting to fake up a *residence de tourisme* to get in on this act. My advice is against it. It is too complicated. You need to be a real live French developer for this. He can play the game exactly and precisely by the book.

VAT can also be relevant to a hands-on rental operation. If you provide what is called 'para-hotel services' (*prestations de para-hôtellerie*) – that is to say breakfast, regular cleaning of the premises, the supply of linen and the reception of guests – you can charge the guests VAT at the reduced rate of

5.5 %, from which you can deduct the VAT paid on your purchases. You will at first need a bookkeeper for this purpose. This is because the reduced rate only applies to the price of the room, not the breakfast. If you do not offer para-hotel services, your lettings in France are exempt from VAT.

You do, of course, whether you live primarily in France or not, have to pay French income tax on your rental income. Provided that your rental income is less than 76,000 euros per year you can, and normally should, elect for the micro-business pre-determined system whereby 72% of your gross income is automatically treated as expenses, and you get taxed on the remaining 28%. The income tax paid in France is deductible from your UK charge to tax on the same rentals, calculated in accordance with the less favourable UK computation methods, not the French method.

Do you want to do a runner from all this financial talk? Take a taxi! The words tax and taxi have the same latin root, taxare, which is to appraise the amount of something. Your taxi is so called because it has a taximeter which works out your fare.

# No trust in trusts?

**By Philippe Piedon-Lavaux    May 2006|**

Irrespective of the proposed 2007 budget, changes introduced by Gordon Brown, and the disincentive of using trusts for UK domiciled individuals, those moving to France should still consider the potential impact if they are beneficiaries of a trust or are a trustee. Clearly we will need to look at the details when the Finance Act has been passed.

A French court order dated 4 May 2004 (TGI Nanterre) indicated that a beneficiary of a discretionary trust who was French tax domiciled should not be assessed for French wealth tax on the funds that were held in the trust. This was the first time a court had considered the implications of trusts for calculating wealth tax. It sheds some light on a very grey area of French law.

The case reminded us that France has still not ratified the Hague Convention dated 1 July 1985, which deals with the law applicable to trusts as well as their recognition. In France trusts are frequently seen as a way to facilitate fraud from an inheritance point of view or tax evasion. The lack of legal recognition of trusts has inevitably caused many concerns on the tax side. Those who have a will trust or are setting up a trust before moving should consider it very carefully.

Income received by a trust mainly falls under Article 120-9 of the French Tax Code (CGI). This indicates that 'income' called 'produits' in French, should be taxed when arising from a trust and considered as a dividend arising from shares located offshore from France.

Nevertheless the tax treatment of the trust position in France is still difficult to grasp, due to the lack of recognition and clear understanding by the French Inland Revenue. Most French lawyers call it an 'enigma'. Consequently you should be careful as to the current position, which might change, as most of its effects have not yet been tested in the French courts.

It is important to remember that individuals considered French domiciled under the French tax rules (Article 4BCGI) and under the double tax treaty between France and the UK in relation to income tax, will be subject to a worldwide tax liability in France. On this basis, an individual who is French tax domiciled should make a distinction between pure income, distributed gains, distributed capital and non-distributed income.

Any income distributed by the trust in the hands of the beneficiary will be subject to French income tax. This is irrespective of the form of the trust or origin of the income.

Under Article 120-9 distributed gains arising from a trust should also be considered income and are therefore subject to French income tax.

Capital in theory should remain outside the scope of Article 120-9, as long as it can clearly be distinguished from the income, interest or gains. Complete and accurate accounts will be required to convince the French Revenue. Bear in mind that if the settler of the trust and the beneficiary are not the same, it is likely that a transfer of capital might attract inheritance tax or gift tax if it doesn't fall under the income (*produit*) criteria.

Rollover income that has not been distributed is excluded from Article 120-9 and should therefore not be subject to French income tax. In response to income or gain which was not distributed, and therefore not subject to tax in France, the 1999 French budget introduced a new Article 123 bis CGI, in order to tax such income located offshore (i.e. outside France in a place considered to have a better tax treatment). Broadly, its conditions are as follows:

• The beneficiary of the trust must be French tax domiciled at the time when the trust acquires the income.

• This applies to trusts and foundations as well as any other legal or corporate structures which have their own legal entity.

• The trust would need to contain more than 50% of stocks and shares, funds or credit.

• The country where the trust is located must be considered as having a better tax treatment than France for a corporate structure under Article 238a; it is generally recognised that a difference of at least one-third fulfils the condition.

• The beneficiary needs to hold a minimum of 10% of the shares or rights directly or indirectly (through his family, for example).

However, the view is generally that a beneficiary of a discretionary trust will not fall under Article 123 bis unless the trust documentation can establish with some certainty that the trustees will distribute on a regular basis a certain percentage of the income to the beneficiary. In this case the trust will then lose the qualification of a discretionary trust.

From a legal point of view trustees may purchase in their own name and register the title through the French Land Registry.

In the event the trust is constituted without complying with the French rules of inheritance, the penalty would in principle be the reduction of the trust.

A trust may be disregarded if the heirs deprived of their inheritance rights can establish that this was precisely the intention in constituting the trust. The Caron v O'Dell case is considered to be the main example of this type of attack (*Cour de Cassation,* 1985).

As the concept of the trust does not exist under French law, it is not possible for the legal title of a property to be held directly in trust at the Land Registry in France.

However, it is possible to use an intermediate company, which is itself held in trust. Thus, anyone moving to France on a permanent basis will need to focus on both the legal and tax implications and ensure that the appropriate structure for holding assets or receiving income is in place.

# Buying a flat in a block

## By Phillipe Piedon-Lavaux    June 2006

Buying a flat in an existing block (*copropriété*) can be an intimidating experience in France, and you may be cautious of the rules that apply to the running of the block. It is easy to imagine that the property, as it is in a foreign country subject to a different legal system, may come with complications.

When viewing a flat the purchaser doesn't usually focus on legal issues and the way the legal title is organised. It's only when they have found a suitable property that they query the way it is managed.

Purchasers are required to sign a contract (i.e. *compromis de vente or promesse de vente)* as soon as the offer has been accepted. The contract will be subject to conditions. Assuming these conditions are met, completion will take place. Following the signing of the contract there is a seven-day cooling-off period allowing the purchasers to have second thoughts and giving them a right to withdraw. If the deposit has already been paid it will be returned to them. Prior to the signing of the contract it is important to take into account the regulations of the block of flats and the way it is managed. You should also take a close look at any pending issues before being completely bound by the contract.

In France you purchase the freehold ownership of a flat, cellar, garage or parking space. There is no limitation period and the property can be transferred to forthcoming generations.

### Deed of conditions

As the flat is within a block, a deed of conditions known as the 'réglement de copropriété – état descriptif de division' will have been set up as part of the legal title of the flat. This deed sets out the permitted use, conditions and any limitations in relation to the flats (known as the private parts held freehold by the flat owners) and also common parts used by everybody such as corridors, external gardens and structure of the building.

The document distinguishes in detail the common parts from the parts within the block owned solely by the property owners. It is important to obtain this document as it contains the relevant information with regard to your rights and obligations and also describes the basis upon which the management and maintenance costs will be divided between the owners.

Each flat, garage, cellar or parking space is usually recorded as a unit (*lot*) with a number and a certain amount of shares (*milliemes*), which will be used for assessing any liabilities or costs to be allocated.

### Managing body (syndic)

The *syndic* is an individual or company appointed by and acting for the flat owners. He manages the block on a day to day basis, deals with maintenance issues, works that need to be carried out, repairs, insurance, cleaners, gardeners, litigation against neighbouring properties, and collects flat owners' contribution costs etc.

He has to report to the flat owners and this is usually done on an annual basis during the general meeting where all owners will be asked to attend after having received notice with the agenda.

Any new purchasers should be aware that the *syndic* should have at his disposal a booklet detailing works and litigation issues pending. Unfortunately this is frequently not in place in many blocks.

### Assemblee générale

*Assemblee générale* is the French name given to the meeting that the flat owners attend. It is the body entitled to make major decisions, appoint the chairman, the managing body i.e. *syndic* and deals with any issues involving the block. As indicated, minor issues will usually be dealt with by the *syndic*. Decisions will be made by voting and the percentage of votes required for a decision to be accepted and binding to everyone will depend on its finality.

Decisions involving major changes and in particular affecting the unit's title will require unanimity.

The cost of the works will be apportioned depending on the amount of *milliemes* bearing in mind that the *copropriété i*s not a company but a legal body of another kind.

### Works

If works are to be done to a flat you should look at the block's regulations as some of the work might require the architect's approval who is in charge of the block and also the other flat owners' consent given during the *assemblee générale*. This can be inserted in the initial contract in France as a let-out clause. With regard to the works conducted by the block we would recommend obtaining the last year's or even two years' annual meeting resolutions (*deliberation*) that lay out any works which have been voted and budgeted for the future.

At the time of purchasing a flat it is essential to have an understanding of any works which are pending or planned, and who will undertake responsibility for paying for those works. Contracts usually contain clauses although a vendor will naturally try to pass any liability to the purchaser.

## Surface area

A flat should be measured in accordance with the measurement scheme called 'loi carrez'. The vendor takes responsibility for this and will frequently employ a surveyor to provide the measurements. A claim can be made within one year against the vendor for damages and misrepresentation if the surface area of the flat is less than 5% of the quoted figure.

Again this is not an exhaustive list and we strongly recommend that those who are not familiar with the French system take advice.

# The resale timebomb

**By Sean O'Connor    June 2006**

I have touched on the subject of property resale values before but it is a complicated one and the 'mechanism' has a tougher sting in it than I realised.

Let's say you have bought an old French farmhouse for a song. Now, only six weeks later, you want to resell it at three times what you paid for it. To make the figures simple, you bought it for 100,000 euros and now have a purchaser lined up at 300,000 euros. Can't get better than that? But now French law steps in which says that if after subtracting seven-twelfths of the resale price from that price the resulting figure is more than your initial purchase price, your initial vendor can cancel his sale to you.

To illustrate the point further we will call the initial vendor Monsieur Dupont and your prospective incoming purchaser Mr Brown: seven-twelfths of 300,000 euros is 175,000 euros. Deducting that from 300,000 euros leaves 125,000 euros which is more than the 100,000 euros you initially paid so Dupont can cancel his sale to you. The *notaire* will not sign the sale from you to Brown because Brown would get bad title. Dupont could kick him out.

Under French law this mechanism applies for two years from when you bought from Dupont. The two-year period runs not, as you might think, from the date of the deed of sale signed by Dupont, but from the date when, under the preliminary contract that he signed, all suspensive conditions were met. After the two-year period has expired, you can resell to Brown at any astronomic figure you can persuade Brown to pay. The mechanism no longer applies.

And don't think you can keep the sale quiet, news travels fast in a French village. Dupont hears you have signed a contract for 300,000 euros with Brown and sends you a stinging letter saying he is cancelling his sale to you.

French law lays down what happens next. You can hand the property back to Dupont, in which case Dupont must return to you the 100,000 euros you paid to him, and consequently Brown will have an action against you for breach of contract, the contractual penalty for that breach could supposedly be 10% of 300,000, i.e. 30,000 euros. So on getting back the 100,000 euros from Dupont you then pay out 30,000 euros to Brown. But your woes aren't over yet because even if Brown was supposed to pay the estate agent's commission, French law says you must pay it because you are the person in default. If the commission is 8% of 300,000 euros, bang goes another 24,000 euros – from the 100,000 euros you are left with 46,000 euros. Far from winning a 200,000-euro profit, you have lost 54,000.

But French law does offer another way forward. Instead of taking the resale price as the actual value, you can appoint a valuer to discover what the true value of the property was on the date of the sale to you. However, I will assume the true value is the same as the re-sale price you have agreed with Brown. French law says you can see off Dupont by paying him a make-good price calculated as shown. In this calculation P = the price you paid Dupont. V1 = the true value as at when you sold to Brown. V2 = the value at the time when you offer to pay the make-good sum. As I said, in my example below, V1 and V2 are the same.

So you pay another 170,000 euros to Dupont and complete your onward sale to Brown. Your total outlay to Dupont is 270,000 euros and your profit therefore 30,000 euros. Well played!

I have ignored fees, costs and capital gains tax. The whole scenario is complicated and a lawyer should be consulted.

# Le legacy nouveau est arrivé

**By Sean O'Connor    August 2006**

From 1 January 2007, the French inheritance laws will undergo a fairly radical shake-up – the new law introducing the changes was adopted on 14 June 2006. I will concentrate on three major changes here.

• At present your child cannot renounce his compulsory forced heirship rights until after you have died. However, from 1 January 2007 your children will be able to assign their compulsory rights to someone else, provided that the deed of assignment is signed by two *notaries,* one acting for you and one for the children. The assignee can be another of your children or your second wife, for example.

Thus if you have two children by a previous relationship and one by your second marriage, the two children will be able, if they agree, to assign their compulsory rights to your second wife if she survives you, or to the child born of your second marriage if she does not. The two children may be willing to do this if you offer to compensate them out of your UK assets, for example.

The assignment of rights need not apply to the whole of a child's entitlement. For example, if you have two houses in France, it will be possible for your children to sign up to an assignment of rights in respect of one house, not the other.

The forthcoming change in the law will not help you if, for example, one of your children has not seen you for 20 years and refuses to have anything to do with you. The forced heirship rights have not been abolished. You would have to find that child and persuade him to agree to an assignment, which he probably would not want to do.

• With effect from 1 January 2007 it will be possible for your French will to lay down what is to happen to your house after your children have died. Thus if you have one child who in turn has three young children (your grandchildren), you can leave your French property to your child on the condition that he keeps it and leaves it to your grandchildren.

Your will won't be able to specify that your grandchildren keep the property for their children or for anyone else. In other words, you can only tie up the property for one generation.

Will your child be obliged to maintain the property in good condition? The answer is yes, because the new law says that you can lay down obligations in your will binding your son on these matters.

• You will also be able to leave your French property to your son in your will as long as he hands it on to his three children – but here comes the twist. Your son need not, assuming your will goes down this route, maintain the property and need not keep all of it.

Thus if your son sells off a few fields and allows the house to deteriorate, then when he dies your grandchildren simply take the collapsed property minus the sold-off fields. Your will can stipulate that your son is not to give any of the property away, so if he wants to reduce the size of it piecemeal, he must sell bits of it off. The main point here is that your son cannot leave any of the property to anyone else in his will, so your grandchildren must receive what is left. Does your son have to keep any of the property at all? This is not clear, but it seems that the answer is no.

The new law runs to 51 pages, so I have only picked out the main points here. I may come back to this matter when I have digested it more. The whole scene is evidently becoming more complicated, so I expect that means a lot more work for French property lawyers like me!

# Planning life assurance

## By Philippe Piedon-Lavaux    August 2006

Life assurance is a general term which in practice covers many different kinds of life contracts in France. The contracts are called 'assurance-vie' and are seen more as financial products than simple contracts insuring against death. Part of their success was the advantageous tax breaks they provided but in recent years the tax advantages have been partly reduced. However, you should consider life assurances when tax planning. In some cases it will be used as a financial product providing an income – some might find it attractive for providing a pension, for example, whereas for others it could be an attractive estate planning tool.

In France there are three main groups of assurance contracts: first, assurance in case of life, which will help to build savings and wealth; second, assurance in case of death, which will secure capital in case of a death; and third, a mixed assurance with the aim of building some savings and securing capital in case of death.

The contract itself is usually divided into two sections – the first describes the general conditions of the contract and the second lays out the characteristics of the product. In some contracts only one premium (*prime*) will be paid, in others payments will be made at agreed stages. Signatories will be given a 'note of information' which provides a 30-day pulling-out period from the day the first premium was paid.

Financial advisers, insurance companies and banks can explain and guide you through the different types of contracts, and help you decide which one is the most suitable for your circumstances and financial needs. However, the tax position and the inheritance impact should be considered.

From a legal point of view anyone intending to move to France should consider these contracts as a savings management tool to generate an income, transfer assets to a partner or down to the next generation. This is particularly relevant when diversifying wealth among properties, investments and financial products. Life assurance contracts are commonly used in inheritance and estate planning and are part of an individual's overall wealth. It is crucial to review any wills at this time.

If a beneficiary's name is indicated in the life assurance contract this might trigger an issue if this is know by the said beneficiary. The beneficiary's acceptance will by law freeze the benefit of the contract.

Unless he waives his acceptance and gives his consent, the contract cannot be allocated to any other beneficiary. In order to prevent this it is advisable to keep the beneficiary's name secret or insert a clause indicating that the beneficiaries will be nominated in a will or in a separate beneficiary's clause lodged with a lawyer or financial institution. The beneficiary's acceptance may have some advantages however. From an estate planning point of view it might be classed as a gift. You could also provide a guarantee to a bank nominated as the beneficiary instead of registering a charge against a property, which is always more expensive in France. Finally, for inheritance tax or wealth tax planning, it can be argued that the acceptance by the beneficiary (freezing the contract for his benefit) should then remove the value of the life assurance contract from the subscriber's estate or wealth tax.

It is possible to indicate that on the policy holder's death its benefit should be passed to one beneficiary (quasi-usufruit), which could be the surviving spouse, for example, and the children in capital as the ultimate beneficiaries subject to the surviving spouse's quasi-usufruit. This will manage both the children and the surviving spouse's interests.

On death the surviving spouse will be entitled to the life assurance contract and on his or her death the predeceased spouse's children will have a claim against the surviving spouse's estate for the capital which is left. This will come as a debt in the surviving spouse's estate exempt from inheritance duties. The policy holder could stipulate that the surviving spouse will be exempt from giving any guarantee to the ultimate beneficiaries. On the other hand French law states under article 1094-3 of the Civil Code the right for the beneficiaries to ensure that the capital is lodged somewhere as a guarantee (*emploi des sommes*).

From a French inheritance law point of view, the life assurance code (article L 132-13) provides that the funds paid as a consequence of a life insurance contract are outside the subscriber's estate.

The highest French court (*Cour de Cassation*) confirmed on the 23 November 2004 that contracts securing the differed payment of capital (*contrat de capitalisation or assurance-vie à capital différé*) should be considered as life assurance contracts as long as there was an uncertainty based on life expectancy.

Conscious that life assurance contracts could be used as an unfair way to disinherit beneficiaries entitled to French statutory inheritance rights, the Life Assurance Code also indicates that it is essential to ensure payments of the premium are not 'obviously excessive' in the light of what the policy holder can financially afford.

The date for assessing this criterion is when the premiums are paid, and there are three ways to work out if they are 'obviously excessive': the policy holder's wealth, the amount of income, and the necessity for the policy holder to sign a life assurance contract in the light of his or her age and the presence of children. This criteria is difficult to assess and is largely open to interpretation by the court. Should the court consider the premium was obviously excessive, a fraud is noted and will have to be sanctioned. The beneficiaries, who are entitled to inheritance statutory rights, should have a claim for the amount above what is not excessive against the life assurance beneficiary.

Those who aim to disinherit a child and leave everything to a surviving spouse should be particularly careful. Schemes such as marriage contracts could help to overcome this threat, although those having children from a previous relationship are likely to remain exposed.

The French rules of domicile and inheritance do not only apply to properties. Getting independent legal advice could also prove to be as essential to the financial assets and investments, which are likely to be subjected to the same principles.

# When a let isn't a let

## By Sean O'Connor    September 2006

It sometimes happens in France that you have purchased more land with your property than you actually need so it seems sensible to allow a local farmer to make use of it. Therefore if you are accepting rent it is sensible to make such a deal legal before you hand over the land.

First if you are accepting rent you have created an agricultural tenancy such that the farmer can keep the land for his lifetime, and his children for their lifetime after that. Rent, for this purpose, can be in cash or in kind – beware of accepting a few sheaves of wheat, for example.

Make sure you pay the land tax and don't allow your gardener to have a patch for his own vegetables. In a recent case it was upheld that the gardener's activities in the garden constituted 'rent' for his patch. If you fall ill, don't let the farmer call the doctor or take you to hospital. There have been cases where this 'good' deed has been deemed to be the farmer's rent.

Second, you can, and should, sign a contract with the farmer if you are making the land available without rent. This constitutes a specific sort of contract in French law governed by Articles 1875-1891 of the French Civil Code. It is called a lending for use law (*un prêt à usage*). Article 1876 says that the loan is specifically without charge (*essentiellement gratuit*) and the lender remains the owner of the land let.

The borrower is required, by Article 1880 of the Civil Code, to look after the land in a 'husbandlike' manner (*en bon père de famille*). If he fails to do so, he will be liable to you for damages. The borrower must use the land for the purpose agreed in the contract and if the land deteriorates because of that use the farmer is not liable to you for any deterioration.

If the farmer has had to incur some extraordinary and unexpected expense in order to maintain the land, he can claim it off you.

If you owe the farmer money for any reason – perhaps you have bought a car off him but have not yet paid for it – this does not constitute a basis for the farmer remaining in occupation of the land after the expiry of the period laid down in the contract. He must give the land back.

The contract will be for a specified period, for example one year, or until the harvest has been brought in. In normal circumstances you can't demand the land back until the agreed period has expired. However Article 1889 of the Civil Code says that if you need to retake possession of the land for some urgent and unforeseen reason, the court can order the farmer to hand it back to you.

If the land presents a danger to the farmer that you are aware of but conceal from him, for example if the land is polluted, you will be liable to pay him damages.

Generally, such a contract is short and simple. You should have it drawn up by the *notaire* through whom you purchased your property since he holds the original of your title deed. This won't be an expensive job. The wording of the document is technical, so you should not attempt to do it yourself, particularly since the consequences of falling into an agricultural tenancy are so drastic and horrendous.

The agricultural tenancy legislation does not apply to any genuine gardening situation. This is expressly stated in Article L.441 – 2 of the Rural Code, and it is not the gardener who pays you. On the contrary it is you who pays him!

# VAT on French property

**By Philippe Piedon-Lavaux    September 2006**

In France VAT is payable on new property transactions, whereas older properties attract stamp duty. You may also have to pay VAT on building work. This tax can also have an implication when you come to sell the property.

### VAT and stamp duty

In France transactions for resale property over five years old are subject to stamp duty (*droits d'enregistrement*). The amount of duty varies depending on the type of property and where it is located. It contains the following taxes:

• 3.6% for the 'departement'. This rate varies depending on the location and type of property from 1% to 3.6%.

• 1.2% for the 'commune' or village where the property is located.

• 2.5% for the state based on the departement's tax.

• 0.1% or 0.2% for the state depending on whether the property is subject to the normal or a special rate.

When buying a property it is important to remember that on top of the stamp duty or VAT, the *notaire's* fees and disbursements will be an added expense unless the vendor is taking responsibility for all purchase costs, in which case the clause relating to the price should indicate that the purchaser is buying 'acte en mains' (including costs).

According to Article 257, 7 of the French tax code (CGI), VAT at a rate of 19.6% applies to newly constructed or delivered property, i.e. the first sale. This covers the following transactions:

• The sale of a building plot, excluding those sold to individuals building a domestic dwelling which will remain subject to stamp duty. VAT will apply to those buying through a company, for example, or building commercial premises.

• The sale of a property off-plan. There were an estimated 70,000 sales off-plan in 2005.

• The sale of a property built less than five years ago which has not been sold before to someone who was not a developer or professional.

When VAT is payable the sale is either exempt from stamp duty or subject to a reduced stamp duty rate of 0.715% for off-plan properties.

The sale of a building plot for dwelling use is not subject to VAT irrespective of the size of the land. The property can be used as a main or second home even when an existing property has to be renovated *(réhabilité)* in which case the sale is then subject to stamp duty. The purchase of land for the construction of a new commercial building, or the purchase of an existing uncompleted building will fall under the VAT rules.

It is important to note that the purchase of a property which has been completely renovated or converted is generally subject to stamp duty, not VAT, unless the amount of work is so extensive it could be considered a new property. The purchaser will have to build within four years to retain the benefit of the VAT scheme, otherwise the sale will revert to stamp duty and the purchaser won't be able to recover or offset VAT already paid on purchase, or on the works and materials.

Properties sold off-plan are subject to VAT. Some developers put properties on the market with a VAT rebate scheme, but to get the VAT refund these properties have to be let commercially subject to conditions.

Properties sold for the first time less than five years after the works have been completed remain subject to VAT. The VAT is payable by the vendor although it is included in the purchase price.

**VAT and works on property**

Most works carried out on domestic dwellings attract 5.5% VAT, subject to conditions. This reduced rate (rather than 19.6%) applies only if the property is more than two years old, habitable or occupied when the works start. All property owners can receive this rate – individuals, corporate structures, tenants and anyone with the free use of the property, which could be a main or second home. It can be a flat or a house, but commercial or professional properties are excluded.

The 5.5% VAT rate can also be achieved where a change of use from professional to domestic dwelling is planned. This applies to works involving improvements *(améliorations)*, conversion *(aménagement),* maintenance *(entretien)* and the fitting of some equipment.

The works have to be carried out by a professional and invoiced directly to the client. Architect's fees in relation to these works will also be subject to the reduced rate.

**Tax on sale**

VAT paid on purchase might have an impact for those reselling a new-build property. Should they resell within five years the transaction could still remain subject to VAT. The vendor will pay VAT on the gain as he can only offset the VAT he paid on the purchase and on costs.

In addition French capital gains tax, and eventually tax representative costs, will also apply. Those selling and relying on the proceeds of sale should not underestimate this.

Anyone purchasing a building plot, an off-plan property or a new-build should not overlook the VAT element. Some will see it as an opportunity to purchase the property under a VAT rebate scheme. Those who intend to let the property with added services might structure their investment in a way which will allow them to claim back the VAT.

# Fingers crossed for planning permission

## By Sean O'Connor    October 2006

Is it going to be your dream house? Are you going to be able to make the conversions and extensions you would like? The contract, which in the French system is signed as it were on day one, can be subject to a suspensive condition relating to obtaining outline planning permission. Here then are the basics on how the outline planning system works in France.

The application has to be lodged at the local *mairie* (town hall) on the official form. Normally the *notaire*, estate agent or land surveyor submits it on behalf of the owner. Permission is supposed to be issued within two months from the date of lodging, but often this does not happen in practice. You may have to wait for three months or more.

The form has a space for you to describe the subject matter. It says you can enclose any further documentation you consider necessary for the understanding of your project. Thus it may be desirable to include sketch plans, at least, of what you want to do, and where you want to put it, but none of this is essential.

The outline permission is called a 'certificat d'urbanisme'. This can be positive or negative, i.e. the answer to the question can be yes or no. Therefore it is important to check the certificate issued is positive.

The outline permission will consider whether the commune has a land development plan or not. If it does, the maximum permitted constructible surface area on the plot will be stated, as will the surface area of existing constructions, hence the outstanding permitted constructable surface area available for future constructions. Whether there is access from the public road, and the availability of drinking water, drainage and electricity will all be considered.

Any specific requirements governing permission will be stated. For example: "Construction projects shall be of traditional type and must look similar to existing constructions so as not to have any adverse effect on the character of the surroundings. Any architectural project typical of any other region will be refused. The project shall be submitted to the opinion of the architect advising the commune." Or "since the land is not served by a public drainage system, a septic tank must be installed. A demand for an authorisation concerning the septic tank must be lodged at the *mairie* prior to the lodging of the application for building permission. The septic tank must be compliant with the requirements of the regulations in force".

The date on which the outline permission is issued is stated. This is significant because it is valid for one year; it is automatically renewable for a second year provided the application for such renewal is lodged within 10 months from the date of issue. Thus if the date of issue is 1 October, the application for renewal must be lodged by 31 August of the following year. This means it must reach the *mairie* by that date, if sent by post, or be personally delivered by hand. The application for renewal has to be made on plain paper in two copies and must be accompanied by the original of the outline permission to be renewed.

The application for building permission itself must be lodged within the period of the validity of the outline permission.

If the application is refused, you can ask the authorities to reconsider their decision. This is called 'un recours gracieux'. Alternatively, you can appeal against the decision to the administrative court, doing so within two months from the date of the decision. This is called 'un recours contentieux'.

A decision handed down refusing permission will always state the reasons on which the refusal is based. Those reasons are normally perfectly logical so you would need expert local advice before appealing.

# A tricky tale of two owners

## By Sean O'Connor    November 2006

Monsieur Dupont was a duplicitous fellow. When he agreed to sell his property to Mr B and signed the contract of sale he had already authorised an estate agent to sell the property to someone else. He didn't tell Mr B or his *notaire*. Mr A seems to have been a bit slow because Mr B's sale went through normally. The deed of sale in Mr B's favour was duly signed and registered at the local Land Registry.

Mr B moved in, furnished the place and spent a lot of money on it.

So it was that a furious Mr A went to the local French court and brought an action against Dupont, and won. The court ruled that his contract was valid and that the judgment should be registered at the Land Registry.

Mr B wasn't made aware of any of this and out of the blue a letter arrived from the *notaire* enclosing the judgment, telling him that Mr A was the official owner of what he thought was his property. Mr B was about to be kicked out of what he thought was his own house.

Next Mr B's *notaire* consulted the legal advisory body to the French notarial profession, the CRIDON (*Centre de Récherche d'Information et de Documentation Notariales),* who looked at the rules concerning land registration. They said that in a conflict between successive purchasers of the same property claiming under the same vendor, the first person to register should take precedence, adding that this rule was only valid in so far as the purchase was made in good faith. The question as to good faith or not was to be considered as from the date of the contract, not the date of the deed.

Mr B was acting in good faith of course. His title was already registered. Mr A's title, consisting of the court judgment, had not yet been submitted to registration at the Land Registry.

The CRIDON also pointed out that there is a system of pre-notation at the Land Registry in France. Thus Mr A could, if he had got wind of the fact that Dupont had sold to Mr B (perhaps he was not actually aware of that at the time), prior to the date of your registration, have lodged a pre-notation consisting of notice of an application to the court for a ruling in his favour at the Land Registry. Then if the court did rule in his favour within three years of that pre-notation, the ruling would be backdated to that of the pre-notation. In this circumstance Mr A would take priority over Mr B.

Thankfully, no such pre-notation had been done. So if Mr A had gone ahead with attempting to obtain registration of his judgment at the Land Registry, the registry would have thrown it out. Mr B need do nothing. Or he could bring an action before the court lodging a so-called third party opposition requesting the court to alter its judgment but on this particular occasion Mr B can keep his cheque book in his pocket and not bother to go to court. He has come through unscathed.

There is a Latin maxim for all of this: qui prior est tempore potior est jure – he who is first in time is stronger in law. We have exactly the same principle in English law.

# Searches in France

**By Christophe Dutertre   November 2006**

One of the characteristics of property transactions in France is the vendor's lack of responsibility regarding the state of the property. Article 1643 of the Civil Code can exempt the vendor of any warranty and the *notaire* will not hesitate to use it to prevent any litigation after completion.

The purchaser has to be careful before committing to a binding contract. Unlike in the UK where a survey will be carried out on the property, the purchaser under French law will buy the property as seen and may struggle to obtain compensation before the court should a problem arise after completion.

However, the legislator, conscious of the problem, has introduced a variety of regulations forcing the vendor to give the purchaser minimum advice and details in the form of reports and surveys on different aspects of the property. The introduction of the asbestos regulations were formalised in 1996; termites and lead followed in 1999, and most recently in 2005 the *dossier de diagnostic technique* (DDT) was created which will be released on 1 November this year. In one document the DDT will contain reports and surveys on asbestos, lead, termites, gas installation, natural and technological risks and energy performance diagnosis.

Before signing any contract the property owner will have to provide the purchaser with a DDT containing the following information:

• **Lead poisoning**: A report on lead poisoning should be provided for any property built before 1 January 1949. The survey must measure the amount of lead present in any surface of the property such as doors, windows, shutters and balconies. The report will be valid for one year and should be attached to the initial contract.

• **Asbestos**: The legislation applies to any building (domestic dwelling, condominium block and commercial premises) where planning permission was granted before 1 July 1997. The vendor is responsible for providing the report which should be prepared by a professional who will locate the presence of asbestos in the property and the state of conservation. The professional, who should be guaranteed by an insurance company, will inform the owner of any potential risk and treatment which should be carried out on the property. Acknowledgement of this report before signing a contract is important as the parties may have to determine the cost of any treatment that may be required.

• **Termites**: Termites are present in more than half of the departments in France from Paris to the south. The survey will only be compulsory in an area identified by the local authorities. Like the other surveys, the report should be attached to the initial contract and must be dated less than three months before the signing of a final contract. For instance, a report provided at the signing of the initial contract will have to be renewed if completion at the *notaire's* office does not take place within three months. It is also important to understand that the legislation only refers to termites, and the presence of any other woodworm such as *vrillettes* (furniture beetle) will exempt the vendor from any responsibility.

• **Natural gas**: If the property has gas installed more than 15 years ago, the vendor will have to provide a report informing the purchaser of any potential risk regarding the installation.

• **Natural and technological risks**: These regulations came into force on 1 June this year. Recent purchasers may already have noticed a new A3 form attached to the initial contract called an 'Etat des risques naturels et technologiques'. The form, completed by the vendor at the local *mairie*, informs the purchaser of two aspects of the property. First it identifies the potential risk covered by a natural or technological prevention plan on the property in the commune. For instance, properties in the Alps are likely to be subject to avalanches or flooding, and properties in the south-east by forest fires. Second, the vendor should also reveal any compensation received from an insurance company as a result of a natural disaster which has affected the property in the past. For instance, reference can be made to the flooding catastrophy that hit the south of France a few years ago.

• **Energetic performance diagnosis**: A vendor will have to advise the purchaser of the energy consumed in the property (the law is still unclear, and it is difficult to appreciate who will be able to carry out this survey and how the report will be set out to inform the purchaser of the energy consumed in the property for a fixed period).

All these reports should be provided before the signing of any contract, in particular the initial contract (*compromis de vente*) signed at the *notaire's* office or at the estate agent's. It is important to make sure the reports are complete before committing to a transaction because any get-out conditions in the contract may not always turn in your favour should a problem arise before completion.

It is probable French legislators will introduce more obligations for the vendor in the next few months and that a further survey regarding electric installations and septic tanks will be added to the exhaustive list.

# Offre d'achat

## By Philippe Piedon-Lavaux    December 2006

Buyers who want to sign a contract to purchase a French property usually start the process through an estate agent. Once you have found the right property you can start negotiating the price. It is fair to try to reduce the asking price by making an offer to the vendor, either verbally or in writing – especially in light of the increase in property prices during recent years and the slowdown of the property market.

The buyer might send a letter to the vendor confirming that he offers an asking price, or the estate agent could ask the purchaser to sign an offer to purchase called an 'offre d'achat' which they pass to the vendor. Both procedures are common practice.

A letter accepting an offer will be regarded as a binding contract between you and the vendor. You must therefore sign this document with care.

An *offre d'achat* is regulated by the general rules of contract law under the French Civil Code and case precedents. It is a unilateral document made by one person (i.e. the buyer) to inform others of his willingness to perform a contract subject to conditions at a certain price.

The *offre d'achat* you will be required to sign might not include any conditions or let-out clauses. You may mistakenly believe it is only a preliminary step prior to the signing of a contract (i.e. the *compromis de vente*). This is where you have to be careful as once accepted by the vendor, your proposal can commit you to the purchase. Both parties will be deemed to have agreed the terms and conditions of the transaction. The vendor would then instruct his *notaire* to proceed and conduct the searches in order to conclude the transaction if the *offre d'achat* makes the parties' intentions clear.

The *notaire* will prepare the transfer of the ownership and draft a title deed (*the acte de vente*). This situation can be unfortunate for a buyer who thought he was entering into further negotiations with the vendor, but ended up committed to the transaction and required to complete at the *notaire's* office several weeks later.

You might wonder what would happen to any conditions that the purchaser intended to include in a contract? It would be too late to request any additional clause as the vendor will be entitled to refuse to sign a *compromis de vente* as he has already accepted, and agreed, the terms of the sale. Only the statutory finance let-out clause for obtaining a mortgage would still apply for the benefit of the purchaser.

The only circumstance in which an *offre d'achat* from the purchaser would not form a binding contract is if the offer contained conditions. Such a document would be considered as a proposal to conduct negotiations without binding the parties. The vendor could also refuse the *offre d'achat* and send a counter offer to the purchaser who would then become the recipient of a new offer. A clear acceptance from the purchaser would then bind the parties to the transaction.

When the recipient receives the offer it creates a situation which varies depending on the wording of the offer. If the offer indicates a validity period for accepting it, the person making the offer is bound during that period and cannot withdraw. If there is no such period the rules set out by a recent court case give the recipient a 'reasonable period of time' during which he can accept if he wants to proceed.

What might appear to be a straightforward offer to sign should be looked at with care. This is particularly true for those who require specific conditions for the conveyance, such as a clause confirming that works done on the property had proper planning consent or that declaration of the works was lodged with the local authorities.

The wording of the offer will also have an impact on the legal implications, as 'I offer to purchase...' may commit you to the purchase whereas 'I am retaining the right to agree' allows for the negotiations you have started to continue without any commitment.

# Rights of the step-children

**By Sean O'Connor    January 2007**

You and your husband purchased a property in France jointly. Your husband had children by a previous relationship. French wills were made. Now your husband has died and you are holding a life interest in his half of the property, meaning that his half will go to his children when you subsequently die.

In French you are the 'usufruitière' of your husband's half i.e. life tenant, and you hold the 'usufruit', meaning life tenancy. Your husband's children are the 'nu-propriétaires'.

I will now look at your rights and obligations in this situation.

You can keep the property for your lifetime. Your husband's children must wait. They can froth at the garden gate, but they cannot come in without your consent.

If you want to sell, you can. They can't stop you. Note, however, that it would be otherwise if your husband had owned all the whole of the property: in that case you could not sell without the children's consent. In the situation here, however, you purchased half each, so you can force a sale. The signature of the children is in principle necessary, but if they refuse to sign, you can apply to the local French court for an order appointing someone else to sign on their behalf.

Upon selling, you must hand over half of the sale proceeds to the children, minus the value of your life interest in your husband's half. The older you get, the less the value of your life interest.

What happens when heavy cracks emerge in the ceiling of the lounge and the walls? The children have to pay for half of the repairs because you are the owner of half (the half you started with), and they are the owners of the other half, subject to your life interest. Some of the light bulbs stop working and a few taps start leaking. This sort is a so-called 'tenant's repair', for which you are responsible. Generally you have to maintain the property and stop it from deteriorating. In principle, half the furniture belonged to your husband so the children now own it, but you can use it all to your heart's content, and if it deteriorates that's bad luck for the children.

You have to pay the whole of the *taxe d'habitation* because you live in the property. The children are supposed to pay half the land tax, because they are, as I have already said, the owners of half the property.

When you die, your life interest will be valued at zero for French inheritance tax so none will be payable. Note that it would be otherwise if the persons waiting to inherit upon your life tenancy coming to an end were your own children. In that case inheritance tax would be payable. This is a point to watch in the case of expensive properties, and in that situation a so-called right of use and habitation, which is almost the same thing as a fully-fledged *usufruit* will be advisable.

There are some lovely apple trees in the garden. Plenty of apple pie for you, because you can use all the apples. The children don't get any of them.

What about the wine your husband left in the cellar? You can drink it but you must leave the same amount of wine of the same quality to the children at your death. If you don't, they can claim the value of it from your estate.

# Are you safe with SAFER?

## By Sean O'Connor    February 2007

If you are buying agricultural land in France, the local agricultural co-operative called a SAFER will normally have a right of compulsory purchase. If the land being sold to you is less than a minimum surface area, the right does not apply. The minimum varies from region to region, but as a rough rule of thumb if the land you are purchasing consists of more than one and a half acres, the SAFER's right probably does apply.

If it applies, the *notaire* handling your transaction must, upon receiving the text of the *compromis de vente* (preliminary contract), give notice to the SAFER of the intended sale to you, mentioning the price. The SAFER then has two months within which to reply. If it does not reply within that period, it is deemed to have waived its right, and the sale can go ahead.

For a small fee in the order of €100, you can get the SAFER to issue a specific reply within one month from notification to it of the intended sale to you.

The expression SAFER is short for 'Société d'Aménagement Foncier et d'Etablissement Rural'. This is hard to translate but roughly it means a company for land development and for the establishing of farmers in business. There are different SAFERs for different areas of France, which sometimes are (and sometimes are not) the same as the administrative geographical departments.

A SAFER is governed by the Rural Code (Articles L.141-1 et seq.). Its statutes must provide that at least one quarter of the members of its board of directors consists of representatives of the regional and municipal councils in its area of activity. The SAFER may receive financial aid from the state in the form of subsidies and loans, but in practice your local SAFER will be strapped for cash. So normally the right of compulsory purchase will only be exercised if there is a local farmer who wants to buy the land to which your contract relates, and who is willing to match the price on your contract.

The SAFER does not necessarily have to match your price. It can take the view that your price is artificially high by local standards, and in that case it can put in its own offer at its own lower price, but the vendor does not have to accept it.

The objects of the SAFER are laid down in Article L. 143-2 of the Rural Code and include the installation, reinstallation or maintenance in situ of farmers, the battle against land speculation, the preservation of the family character of farmholdings, and the conservation of the viability of existing farms where this is jeopardised by the selling off separately of pieces of land and of farm buildings including farmhouses.

Although these objects may sound somewhat old fashioned, in my opinion the local SAFER is a force for social good. The intelligent use of farming land is an important issue for us all. The SAFER seldom pre-empts in my experience. On the other hand, in the few instances where I have acted for a UK farmer purchasing a farm in France, I have found the SAFER to be both helpful and useful. I should add that your contract will always contain a clause whereby if the SAFER pre-empts, your transaction is void and your deposit is returned to you. In the meantime you have to await the SAFER's decision – don't count your chickens before they are hatched is a good agricultural proverb here.

# Buying to let

### By Philippe Piedon-Lavaux    February 2007

Purchasing a buy-to-let property or renting out an empty property in France may be a tempting proposition – the running costs can be covered by letting which can also provide a stream of income. The rules of the French Lease Act, 6 July 1989, which regulates leases of unfurnished properties, are statutory, but the law does not apply to seasonal, commercial or furnished lettings. These rules should be carefully considered before letting a property – a tenant who does not pay his rent or who is difficult might seriously affect the use or the value of the property.

### The lease

The lease must be in writing and should indicate all the names of the parties involved, the lease period, date for receipt of rent (date from which the tenant takes over the property), deposit (which should not be more than two months' rent) and terms and conditions of payment (the amount of the rent and on what terms it can be increased), a description of the premises and its proposed use (i.e. dwelling, dwelling and professional use).

The normal period of a lease is three years if the landlord is an individual or six years if the landlord is a company. However, it is possible to have a lease agreement for more than three years and up to a maximum of 99 years. In exceptional circumstances, such as if a professional or family matter affects the conditions, the duration can be reduced to one year which would allow an early repossession.

If there is a clause in the contract the rent can be reviewed every year. Any increase cannot be more than the rental index, which is published by the French authorities. Should any work be carried out on the premises, the landlord may decide to increase the rent following the completion of the work. Should he want to increase the rent by more than that stated in the previous contract, the landlord can ask the tenant to sign a new lease. The new rent can be increased to bring it in line with the rental price of a similar dwelling in the same town, but the landlord must prove the amount is in accordance with the local market.

If the tenant fails to pay the rent, the landlord may have a number of contractual solutions available to him. He can ask for a third party to act as guarantor should the tenant not be able to pay the rent. Additionally, he can insert a clause stating that the lease is automatically void if the tenant fails to pay the rent or the deposit. However, even in such cases, a court order will still be needed – the landlord sends an injunction notice to the tenant to pay. If after two months the tenant has failed to pay, the landlord can bring a claim through the court. Should the tenant repay the rent arrears within the timescales specified by a judge, the lease cannot be terminated; if the tenant fails to pay, the lease can be terminated, unless the judge grants further time.

During the lease the landlord cannot terminate the contract unless:

• He wants to sell the property empty, in which case he must give the tenant first refusal to buy it. If the tenant can't or doesn't want to exercise his right to buy the property within the two months' notice period, the landlord can then sell it to another purchaser. The tenant's preemption right only applies to a sale or exchange, and the landlord is free to dispose of his property as a gift.

• The landlord, his spouse, or his ascendant/descendants, his/her French civil partnership's partner, decides to live in the property, in which case the dwelling must be used as a primary residence.

• The landlord has 'legitimate and serious grounds' not to continue the lease with the tenant (i.e. if the tenant does not comply with his obligations as defined in the lease); this includes the requirement to carry out major renovation work which can't take place while the tenant remains in the premises and the non-payment of rent by the tenant.

To terminate the lease the landlord must notify the tenant at least six months before it ends and it is preferable to give notice through a bailiff. If the tenant is over 70 years old, and his yearly income is less than 1.5 times the French minimum wage (SMIC), the landlord can't terminate the lease until accommodation complying with the tenant's needs is found in the same area. This does not apply if the landlord himself is more than 70 years old or if his annual income is less than 15 % of the minimum salary.

It is important to understand that the law protects the tenant more than might be expected. Evicting a sitting tenant can take a few years as a court order will be needed – in a recent case it took 16 years to evict a tenant! The tenant, however, can terminate the lease at any time during the agreement. Generally he must inform the landlord by recorded delivery letter three months before the end of the lease. However, there are exceptions when the tenant may leave within a month. Tenants are well protected in France. The current requirements imposed by landlords – guarantors, deposit, bank's guarantee – underline the dysfunction of a system where both interests are not equally preserved.

## The property

Gas and electricity must be safe and in a good state of repair as well as being well ventilated. The property must be well lit with heating and water. If the property is in a condominium, the landlord must provide the tenant with the rules of the building. The tenant must insure the property (*assurance locative*) and must prove he has done so. The landlord must also insure the dwelling (*assurance proprietaire non occupant*).

An inventory (*état des lieux*) is compulsory. It can be performed by both parties or by a bailiff and   must be carried out before the start and at the end of the agreement. Two copies of the inspection results must be provided to both parties and be signed by them. The report must detail the state of the property and provide a list of fixtures and fittings which are rented as part of the agreement, for example the bathroom and kitchen, the state of the external parts, and so on. At the end of the lease, the tenant must hand over the property to the landlord in the same state as when he took it over, allowing for wear and tear and any 'act of God'. Should one of the parties refuse to acknowledge the *état des lieux,* then the property is presumed to be in a good state.

According to law, the tenant cannot sub-let without the landlord's authorisation. If the tenant goes ahead without his permission, then the landlord can demand termination of the lease. It is important to note the lease is personal and cannot be transferred to another person.

# Deal or no deal?

By Sean O'Connor    March 2007

### Reader's query

*I noticed that my roof timbers needed treating for woodworm and contacted two contractors in France with a view to do the work. One was much cheaper than the other so I signed a contract with him and paid a deposit. A few weeks later the first, more expensive builder contacted me saying he had been to the house, done the work and when could he expect payment! I had signed no contract with him and no money had changed hands. When the second builder arrived to do the work, he found the first builder had not only done a botched job but had entered through a broken window. Do I have to pay the first builder?*

There are two aspects to this matter. Was there a contract at all? If yes, was it properly performed? Article 1101 of the French civil code says that a contract is an agreement whereby a person undertakes to do something. A contract can be oral, and silence can mean acceptance. As an example, you go into a French bar and order a beer. The waiter brings it to you and you drink it. Nothing is said about the price or you agreeing to pay it. There is nothing in writing. Nevertheless, a contract is to be presumed, so when the waiter brings you the bill, you have to pay it.

In this case, the householder telephoned the first builder who quoted a price. A contract consists of an offer and an acceptance and the first builder's quote was the offer. The question is whether the householder accepted the quote. This is a matter of evidence that each of the parties could submit to the local court. However it seems that the householder did not accept the quote because he signed a contract with the second builder and paid him a deposit. Moreover he never arranged for the first builder to have the key to the premises so the first builder climbed in through a window, presumably as a trespasser.

Article 1108 of the French civil code says that the consent of a party to be bound by a contract is essential. In this case no consent at all was given. So the provisions of the civil code concerning the situation where consent is given by mistake do not apply. Article 1110 says that a mistake concerning the identity of a person does not constitute a reason to render the contract void unless that person was the principal reason for the agreement. Thus where a bride standing in the church thinks that the person with whom she is exchanging vows is Monsieur Tintin but in fact it is Monsieur Dupont, the marriage contract is void.

In the reader's case he thought the second builder was going to do the job but to his astonishment the first builder beat him to it. He might think he can claim nullity of the alleged agreement with the first builder under Article 1110 but this is the wrong way of looking at the problem. The householder is not in the bride's position. He never entered into a contract with the first builder believing he was the second builder and never entered into any contract with the first builder at all.

Now it's been established that the householder does not have to pay anything to the first builder it is not necessary to consider the question of whether the householder can withhold payment on the grounds that the first builder did not do the job properly.

# Marriage and the community fund

**By Philippe Piedon-Lavaux    March 2007**

When embarking on the journey to French property ownership, a main consideration should be what happens if one of the purchasers dies. Many people still neglect this issue at the time of the purchase and later face major challenges in terms of French taxes or children's statutory rights.

It is advisable to tackle this before making an investment, in order to assess the impact of the French rules and taxes. Don't lose the inheritance tax battle against the French Inland Revenue! However, it is not too late to adopt a scheme which suits your personal circumstances after the purchase

The French Inheritance Act 2006 has brought about some major changes and improvements, in particular in relation to the drafting of wills. Where there are children, the surviving spouse, even as a named beneficiary, will not be in a position to receive the entire estate. In these circumstances couples should consider signing a prenuptial or post-nuptial agreement and entering a community fund or community of property agreement.

### Is it really the most popular scheme for UK buyers in France?

Such agreements (pre-nuptial or post-nuptial) have been in use in France and other parts of the world for a long time. They could be aimed at securing a surviving spouse against the French statutory rules of inheritance. They enable married couples to express how they wish their assets to be held during marriage and divided in the event of a death or divorce.

A community fund called 'communauté universelle', which can be compared in some ways to a joint tenancy agreement, is a form of marriage contract under French law. Under such a contract spouses can specify that all property acquired or received by a husband and wife during their marriage will be deemed to be communal, belonging to a common fund, 'la communauté', administered jointly and with joint powers over these assets.

### Who can use it?

Although the UK has not ratified the Hague Convention of 14 March 1978, it has been in force in France since 1992. Therefore any couples intending to purchase a property, invest in France or move to France, can sign it. Such an agreement is available to those who are already married and should not be compared to a civil partnership agreement.

## Legal implications

The community fund can specify among other conditions that upon the death of a spouse, the entire fund (i.e. everything the spouses owned jointly) accrues to the survivor. They could also exclude one particular asset or a group of assets from the fund, in which case it will fall under French inheritance rules and tax. In this way, spouses should overcome the effect of the French inheritance rules on the first death (i.e. the compulsory children's inheritance rights).

## Tax implications

Upon the death of a spouse, the entire common fund (i.e. everything the spouses owned jointly) accrues to the survivor (*attribution au survivant*) without any French inheritance tax.

The cost, however, is that French inheritance tax will apply upon the second death on the whole aggregated estate of the surviving spouse. Therefore, any tax-free threshold per parent and per child which was available but has not been used on the first death will only work once on the second death. This is the price to pay to retain freedom over the family assets.

## Full or partial?

In accordance with Article 6 of the Hague Convention, for those who intend to remain non-French domiciled (in the French sense of the word, which means that they won't elect France as their main home both in terms of facts and intention), the fund can apply only to their immoveable assets in France (i.e. the property). It will not affect any other assets. The contract is therefore 'partial' as it covers only part of the assets.

Those who intend to move to France or have already established their domicile there, can set up a full community fund for all of their assets. Also, those who initially decide to enter into a 'partial' community fund, can later renew the exercise and sign an addendum including their other assets after they have established a French domicile. Then it will cover worldwide assets and protect the surviving spouse.

## When does it need to be signed?

To reduce costs the community fund should be signed prior to the purchase of a French property (if used as a second home), or after moving to France (for those who become French domiciled). This partial fund can be set up at any time, even after the purchase of the property. This is helpful to those who were not in a position to sign when they should have done so or who did not receive legal advice at the time of their purchase.

### Children from previous relationships

As the fund accrues to the survivor no estate comes into being on the first death. For this reason the children from a previous relationship are entitled to claim against the surviving spouse (who will be the sole owner of the fund) for that which they should otherwise have received under French law on their parents' death, in other words their French compulsory rights.

This might be dealt with as part of a global arrangement in a will in some other territory, perhaps England if some assets remain there.

Also, since the 2006 Inheritance Act, the child can sign a waiver in France indicating that he won't challenge.

### Where to sign it

The setting up of the community agreement can be signed in the UK with a solicitor. For those with existing properties that need to be transferred into a community fund, it is important to remember that there are normally stamp duty costs, which have been temporarily waived by the French Ministry of the Economy.

We would recommend that for those who wish to adopt this scheme there is no time to wait! The presidential election will come up in the spring and depending on who wins, the French tax environment might change. Note that there should also be no French court procedure costs.

In summary, no-one can deny that marriage contracts are helpful wealth management schemes, among others, bringing advantages that are familiar to those investing in France. However, long-term wealth management planning should not be overlooked, and in particular the transfer to the next generation.

# Aimer sa femme

## By Sean O'Connor    April 2007

Suppose you have a house in France in joint names worth €1m, a house in the UK worth £500,000, and liquid assets of £300,000. You are fiscally resident in the UK. You have two children by your existing marriage and a son by a previous marriage. You are 12 years older than your wife so will probably die first. You would like to arrange that if that happens, your wife will inherit your half of the French property. In other words you want to defeat the French inheritance laws.

Can you choose the so-called 'tontine' clause whereby the survivor takes all? No, you can't, because in French law the tontine clause must be entered in the deed of sale on day one. You cannot insert it afterwards.

Moreover, as you are more than 10 years older than your wife, French law takes the view that the chances of the two spouses dying first are not equal, so that rules out the tontine clause anyway. Even if you did have the tontine clause, upon your death, your wife would have to pay approximately €100,000 in French inheritance tax because, unlike the situation in England, there is inheritance tax between husband and wife.

Can you put the property in the name of a French civil real estate company (*société civile immobilière* or SCI for short)? Yes, you can. The shares in the SCI rank as moveables, which devolve in accordance with the law of the domicile – English domicile so English law. Hence the shares in the SCI can pass to your wife under your English will. But there are problems. Firstly, the French property has gone up in value enormously over the last five years, so you will have to pay French capital gains tax on the transfer to the SCI. Secondly, when you die, the transfer of your shares to your wife under your English will, will be hit with French inheritance tax.

Another possibility is to change your matrimonial regime to a French one. This has two results, firstly that the survivor takes all, and secondly, that no French inheritance tax is payable when the first spouse dies. In other words, by signing up a few papers, you get back to the UK situation. But there is a problem here too. Your son by your first marriage can go to the French court and claim his compulsory reserve. He has 10 years to do so from when you die. His compulsory reserve is four-sixteenths of your half, which is €125,000.

Under the recent changes in French inheritance law, your son can, if he wants, transfer his compulsory rights to your wife, doing so straight away. Then you can change your matrimonial regime. You have solved your problem.

It has to be explained to your son that if you die first, your wife cannot usefully subsequently leave your son anything by will, because your son would pay French inheritance tax at 60% on that gift as he is a stranger in blood to her. So you are asking your son to say goodbye to a future entitlement to €125,000.

Perhaps you could persuade him to do so by giving him a cash gift of £50,000 out of your liquid assets now. Money now is worth more than money in umpteen years time.

Get talking!

# Changes to inheritance tax

## By Philippe Piedon-Lavaux    April 2007

Families might find the new French budget helpful as it solidifies the French Inheritance Act (23 June 2006) and brings more freedom in dealing with estates subject to French inheritance law. This will increase the options available to achieve people's wishes, including the following:

*Gift (*donation-partage*) between generations.

Any child (the donee) who is the beneficiary of a gift can stipulate that his or her own children (i.e. the donor's grandchildren) can be nominated as beneficiaries, and can therefore take their place for part or all of the gift.

*Should the original beneficiary not wish to receive any part of the gift, it won't be considered by the French Revenue as a gift by the original beneficiary if they then pass it to their child(ren). In this way you can bypass the middle generation, allowing them to accumulate the tax-free threshold for each beneficiary.

The beneficiary can receive €50,000 free of tax (above which he would be taxed). In accordance with these new rules, he may then prefer to allocate anything above the tax-free threshold to his own children. For example, a father can gift €80,000 by dividing the amount between his child, who will receive €50,000 tax free, and a grandchild, who will receive €30,000 tax free.

*Gift to a child from a previous relationship.

Any transfer of assets subject to French tax (by death or gift) between non-related individuals is normally subject to 60% tax. However, in the new budget a gift made by a spouse to a stepchild can now cover assets held jointly in both spouses' names (subject to conditions), without attracting a 60% tax rate on half of the assets.

*Tax treatment of waiving inheritance rights.

The inheritance act introduced the right for children to waive their claim under the statutory inheritance rules. This will need to apply to one particular beneficiary and can represent part or the whole of their parent's estate. The waiver is only valid if it is signed in the presence of two *notaires* and incorporates the legal consequences. From a tax point of view, the Revenue will not be able to claim that the waiver is a gift by the child.

*Gradual and residual gifts/ wills.

The inheritance act also introduced new methods giving a donor or a testator some control over the destination of his assets. He could make the following:

(a) Gradual gift or will (*libéralité graduelle*), whereby the recipient has an obligation to keep the property, and upon his death, to transfer it to a further named beneficiary. The second beneficiary will be deemed to have received the assets directly from the initial donor.

(b) Residual gift or will (*libéralité résiduelle*), whereby the recipient is not obliged to keep the property or asset, but must transfer whatever remains upon his or her own death to a further named beneficiary. The budget confirms that on the first death the assets will have to be valued at their market value, or if it is a gift, any allowance in accordance with the donor's age at the time of the gift.

On the second death (i.e. the first beneficiary's death), the second beneficiary will be seen as having received the assets from the initial donor and not from the first beneficiary. However, the assets will be valued on the first beneficiary's death and there will be a tax credit for whatever has already been paid by the first beneficiary. This could be particularly attractive to someone wanting to leave the property to a spouse from a second marriage, but ensuring that the property reverts to their own children.

In the past any transfer from a second spouse to the step-children attracted 60% tax. In this example, the first named beneficiary can be the surviving spouse and the second beneficiary the step-children, who will be considered as having received the assets directly from their own parent (as long as the waiver by the children has been organised).

*Skipping a generation

The new budget finalises the rule introduced in the inheritance act which authorises a child or sibling to pass his rights to their own children and therefore retain the tax allowance they normally would have received (€50,000 for a child, €5,000 for a sibling). In the past a child or sibling who waived their right to be a beneficiary, also disinherited his own children (the share was divided among the remaining beneficiaries). Now the grandchildren will step into their parent's shoes.

Clearly the inheritance act and budget will benefit many families, including:

(a) Siblings waiving their rights for the benefit of a nephew.

(b) Someone who already has substantial wealth and wishes his parent's assets to skip a generation and pass directly to their grandchildren in order to reduce inheritance tax.

**(c)** A waiver from children from a previous relationship which enables the current spouse (step-parent) to receive the assets on their partner's death. The surviving step-parent must transfer the assets on death back to her step-children. For example, Mr and Mrs Smith are married. Mr Smith has a child from a previous relationship. On Mr Smith's death his estate passes to Mrs Smith. The child has waived his claim to an immediate benefit from his father's estate, but Mrs Smith has to transfer the assets to the child on her death.

# Parental Inheritance Rights

## By Philippe Piedon-Lavaux   May 2007

It is unfortunate that most people who move to France tend to postpone inheritance issues until after they have made their investment. This makes it more difficult and costly (and potentially impossible) to achieve what they want.

Despite two recent inheritance acts, children's statutory inheritance rights are still a major feature within inheritance tax planning or estate planning. The recent vote by the French parliament for 'fiducie' – comparable to a trust in the UK – has shown that even with recent legislation, statutory rights will remain in France for the time being. The new acts should give people more flexibility in managing their assets in a way which would be comparable to a UK trust. Nevertheless, provisions have been made to prevent children from being disinherited in the *fiducie* act.

Until 1 January 2007, where there were no offspring French inheritance law required a proportion of property to be left to the surviving parents (which could not be overridden by a will). The only way to supersede parents' rights was to sign one of the nuptial agreements, e.g. *communauté universelle*. From now on, for couples without children, the deceased can bequeath the whole of his estate to his/her spouse. It is essential that a will is drafted (in France or the UK as the Hague Convention 1961 recognises wills in both countries).

Without a will the surviving spouse would receive only 50% of the estate, and each of the parents 25%. If one of the parents has already passed away, the surviving spouse's share increases to 75% of the estate.

Clearly there is a strong incentive to have a will in place, although the spouses may consider entering into a *communauté universelle* which will bring tax exemption in France. The *communauté universelle* can be set up after the couple has moved to France or bought their property.

The Inheritance Act 2006 (introduced from 1 January 2007) compensates parents for the loss of statutory inheritance rights. This right amounts to 25% of any assets gifted by the parents to their child.

If the parents are no longer alive, the surviving spouse receives all of the estate. There are two limits to this. The assets received by the deceased which come from succession or gifts from his parents, and which still exist in his estate, will be divided 50% between his siblings (or their children) and his spouse.

In the event of the deceased spouses' grandparents still being alive (and in need), they can claim against the surviving spouse if he/she has received at least 50% of the estate.

For those dealing with the settlement of an estate subject to French inheritance law, such as executors or solicitors, it will be necessary to take this into account, otherwise a surviving spouse might lose (even with a will) part of the family assets which were received from their spouse's estate.

Always take expert advice when dealing with tax issues.

# Why it's never too late

**By Sean O'Connor    May 2007**

What sort of risk are you taking if the house you are intending to buy has been standing for 25 years but no building permission was ever applied for? If three years or 10 years has lapsed from the completion of the construction no criminal or civil proceedings can be brought. So far so good. On the other hand, if the property burns down, you may not be able to rebuild it.

Therefore you should ascertain whether the land on which the house stands is, under the existing land development plan, constructible. If it is find out what the existing construction coefficient is. For example, if the plot has a surface area of 1,000 metres and the coefficient is 0.5, the maximum surface area that can be built, inclusive of all floors, but excluding uninhabitable attic or basement space, garages, balconies and terraces, is 500m².

Next is the existing house in line with the coefficient. In other words, if you were to apply for the appropriate building permission now, you would get it? If the answer is yes you can apply to regularise the position of the illegal house, but this process will probably take about eight months. The vendor may not be willing to wait that long. In all these circumstances you can buy the house legally 'dirty' and make it legally 'clean' afterwards.

What happens if you want to buy a half-built house and complete the construction works later? Let's assume the building permission was issued in 1998, and the construction works started in 1999 and stopped in 2005 – the building permission was valid for two years, and the works were commenced within time.

The problem here is that the works have been interrupted for more than one year therefore the building permission is no longer valid. Moreover, the certificate of conformity of the half-built construction works with the building permission has not been issued.

You will not be able to complete the works until you get a new building permission, and you will not get that until you have obtained confirmation that the existing works are in conformity with the initial building permission. If they are not in conformity you may have to spend a lot of money putting it right – the half-built kitchen may have to be taken down and put up again.

In this case either employ an architect to examine the existing construction compared with the plans, or simply ask the town hall *(mairie)* to send out an inspector to advise you.

If you still want to go ahead with the purchase, you should render the contract subject to obtaining new building permission bearing in mind that, as is obvious, a half-built house is no use to you.

# High noon at Shadyville

By Sean O'Connor   June 2007

It was in the back office of the estate agency, the place where the stocks of fax-machine paper are kept along with the broom and the dustpan and brush, that you handed over that off-contract cheque for €80,000, purportedly covering the furniture, which in fact consisted of an old tumbledown bed and a few rickety chairs.   The agent, Monsieur Claude Yeuxpartout, promised to keep it in his safe until the sale went through. There would be no problem. After all, what's fifty grand between 'friends'.

Handshakes all round.

In this way, the vendor would pay less capital gains tax and you would pay less in transfer duties. Stuff the taxman. Handshakes all round.

You had signed a contract with Monsieur Leon Renard for the purchase of a half-built villa at a slip of a price. There was a building permission. You would complete the construction works and would soon be swanning around in your plush new quarters.

Monsieur Yeuxpartout had said that you could build another house on the extensive grounds which you could rent out or sell off. That would balance your budget.

The contract, as usual, contained the legally required 'affirmation de sincérité' clause meaning that you declared that the price shown on the contract was the true price, and stating that the parties were informed that there are heavy fiscal penalties for under-declaring the price.

What you had not been told, but subsequently discovered, was that the building permission had expired due to the construction works having been interrupted for a period of more than one year. Moreover the certificate of conformity of the construction works with the building permission had not been obtained. No new building permission enabling you to complete the villa would be issued until the already constructed works had been put into conformity. It was anybody's guess as to how out of conformity they were and as to how much it would cost to put them into conformity.

Then it emerged that the surrounding land was not so extensive in terms of square metres as Monsieur Yeuxpartout had said, so you would never get permission for that second house.

Your budget was now looking heavily over-stretched. You were getting cold feet. You were beginning to panic. And you noticed that the old bed and the chairs had been removed.

Run for the hills...

You consulted a lawyer. He recommended, and so you decided, to withdraw from the sale on grounds of misrepresentation inducing contract, arising because of the silence on the part of Monsieur Leon Renard consisting of non-disclosure of essential information (under Article 1116 of the French Civil Code). Also on grounds of mistake as to the substance of the thing constituting the subject-matter of the contract (under Article 1110 of the French Civil Code).

That cheque for €80,000 had been drawn on your French bank account. Could you trust Monsieur Yeuxpartout? You were not sure. So you decided to transfer those funds back to your UK account quickly.

Then Monsieur Yeuxpartout, acting on instructions from Monsieur Renard, but without informing you, paid in your cheque. Horrors. The dishonouring of a cheque is itself a minor criminal offence in France, with the result that you may no longer use a     bank account.

Moreover the secret arrangement for that off-contract €80,000 portion of the price was about to come out and you were now looking at being hit with heavy penalties for underdeclaring the price. What are those penalties? Three years in prison and €45,000.

You phoned the airport. When was the next flight back to the UK? 18:30. You would be on it. How glad you were when the aeroplane took off.

PS: I hear that old Leon Fox and old Claude Shiftyeyes are now doing their three years in jail.

# Don't overlook wealth tax

## By Philippe Piedon-Lavaux    June 2007

France taxes wealth even if no transfer, death or disposal is involved. The French Finance Act (23 December 1989) re-introduced a wealth tax (ISF) payable by individuals whose total assets value more than €760,000 on an annual basis. This tax is frequently overlooked by those who have invested in France.

Individuals who are not considered as tax domiciled in France are only liable to pay the wealth tax if the net value of their French-based assets is above the €760,000 threshold. For those domiciled in France, their worldwide assets are taken into account.

Properties should be declared at the market value. As the tax is calculated on net assets, existing debts or taxes on 1 January can be offset against the assets for tax purposes. For example, a loan that has been set up for financing a property can be offset (even a loan granted in the UK to buy a French property). Rates vary between 0.55% to 1.80%.

### Living in France?

The concept of domicile is the same as in the context of French income tax. In accordance with the 1968 double tax treaty, a UK domiciled individual will, for example, have a limited tax liability in France, although those who are French domiciled will be taxed on worldwide assets.

The family as a whole will be taxed. For example, the assets of a married couple and any children under 18 years of age will be subject to ISF if they exceed the threshold as a whole, taking into account their aggregated assets.

Only a few exceptions exist in relation to assets, which are not included in the wealth tax basis. The basis of many of these exceptions falls within the business/economic sphere. Antiques over 100 years old, literary and industrial rights, woodland owned and some pensions are also excluded. Properties, contents, boats and even shares (within limits) will be subject to French wealth tax.

For the non-French domiciled, there is a further important exception. Bank accounts in euros or any other currency, stocks and shares and also life insurance are not subject to wealth tax. Subject to conditions, those who commercially let their furnished properties can be exempt from ISF (article 885R CGI).

Those considered as French tax domiciled should lodge their wealth tax form by 15 June. For those domiciled elsewhere in Europe, the deadline is 16 July, and if their domicile is anywhere else in the world it is 31 August.

French wealth tax is due on an annual basis and involves the submission of detailed self-assessment. Failure to declare, or a misleading incorrect self-assessment, both attract substantial penalties imposed by the French Revenue. The Revenue is entitled to impose on taxpayers a French-based representative to deal with these wealth tax formalities.

The effect of the wealth tax should always be considered carefully by those owning property or planning to invest in France, whether they intend to become domiciled there or not. Tax planning advice should always be thought about.

# Rules of the Republique

**By Sean O'Connor    July 2007**

Now that Nicolas Sarkosy has become president of France, let us look at what the French Constitution of 1958, introduced and established by General de Gaulle, says about the president. Directly elected for seven years by vote of the whole population, the president is responsible for:

• Ensuring the Constitution is respected and guaranteeing national independence.

• Appointing the prime minister and dismissing him upon the prime minister submitting the resignation of the government. Upon a proposal from the prime minister, the president appoints the other members of the government and can also dismiss them.

• Taking the chair at meetings of the Council of Ministers (what we would call the Cabinet).

• Promulgating the laws after they have been voted by the National Assembly and the Senate. He can require that a law submitted to him for promulgation be reconsidered. He can in certain circumstances hold a referendum.

• After consulting the prime minister and presidents of the Senate and National Assembly, the president can dissolve the National Assembly.

• Signing orders and decrees adopted in the Council of Ministers.

• Appointing the prefects who represent the government and each geographical department, doing so at a meeting of the Council of Ministers.

• Accrediting ambassadors to foreign countries; ambassadors from other countries are accredited to him.

• The president is the head of the armed forces, and takes the chair at meetings of top-ranking committees handling national defence.

• After consulting the prime minister and presidents of the Senate and National Assembly, and also after consulting the constitutional committee, the president can declare an emergency.

• In criminal cases, the president can exercise what we would call the prerogative of mercy.

• The president can send messages to the Senate and National Assembly which are read, without giving rise to any debate.

**All-powerful leader?**

It emerges from all this that the president is a sort of monarch and prime minister rolled into one. Can he therefore do anything?

In attempting to answer this question, we need to go back to Alexis de Toqueville (1805-1859) who in 1856 published a book called the *Ancien Regime and the Revolution.* In it he demonstrated convincingly that the centralised system of governing France had been established before the Revolution of 1789, and had survived the Revolution.

The prefects sent out from Paris to govern the geographical departments of France have directly replaced the so-called *intendants* that had been sent out by the king, and they do the same job. They constitute the eyes, ears and authority of the central government and implement all administrative matters decided upon by the government.

There is a whole body of administrative law under which the prefects operate and which they enforce. A hierarchy of administrative courts determines the legal relationship between the administration and the citizens. The topmost administrative court is the *Conseil d'Etat* in Paris, which replaced the Conseil *du Roi.*

Theoretically, therefore, the president can do virtually anything, just like the king could. But the administration has its own entrenched procedures, attitudes and ways of doing things. The prefects and other top administrators are all highly intelligent and immensely well-educated, either at the *Ecole d 'Administration* or at one of the other so-called *Grandes Ecoles* in Paris. In reality and in practice, the administration has its own point of view, and it is hard for the president to mess with it.

So is the president really going to be able to abolish inheritance tax as he has said? I am sceptical, but let's wait and see.

# Tax changes to come

## By Philippe Piedon-Lavaux   July 2007

Since the election of Nicolas Sarkozy as the new French President in May 2007, his first measures seem to be in tune with the pre-election promises.

An agenda had already been set up for his first hundred days in office, despite the fact that he would not be in a position to start his new policies before the re-election of a new French parliament in June, which would hopefully give him the majority he needed to drive the reforms France requires.

He and his ministers have already made some announcements on the tax side, moving the country towards a more tax-friendly and market-oriented environment.

### Property ownership

Among the reforms Sarkozy suggested is his proposal to encourage French residents to become property owners of their homes. He indicated that he will give incentives to encourage new constructions and also allow the financial interest for those who need to borrow in order to purchase a property to be offset against the overall household income.

On 24 May the minister in charge indicated that each household will be allowed to offset the loan interests up to 20% of their income. This will apply only to French residents as long as their title deed was signed in front of the *notaire* since 6 May 2007, the date when Sarkozy was elected President. This tax allowance will be limited during a certain period of time, which has not yet been confirmed.

As part of the other proposals which have been made, a minister confirmed the setting up of a tax shield, which will ensure that the amount of tax payable will not exceed 50% of household income. This was particularly damaging for those who are assets rich and cash poor. The current rules put the shield at 60% but don't include the additional 11% tax for social taxes, meaning that the new measure might reduce the tax by 21 points (from 71% to 50%).

With the limitation to 50% this will substantially increase French competitiveness. In Sweden, Spain or Finland the current tax shield is 60%. With this new ruling France will join Germany, which since 1995 has limited its tax shield to the 50% in accordance with a supreme court decision that declared anything above as against the German constitution.

In addition, households who invest in companies (subject to conditions) will receive a tax refund up to €50,000. The new level of tax under the tax shield will continue to undermine the impact of French wealth tax. It is worth mentioning that those who do not complete their wealth tax forms, by indicating that their assets are less than €760,000 and are therefore not subject to wealth tax, are exposed to a 10-year prescription period during which the Revenue can challenge their tax position. Those who have declared a taxable wealth are only subject to a three-year period.

**Income tax**

With regards to income tax, and in order to encourage professionals to work extra hours and bring the country back to work, the government has insisted that working hours above the legal 35 hours a week will have some tax allowances as well as the contributions payable by the employers on these extra hours.

We should hopefully hear of more incentives in the coming weeks, such as VAT at the reduced rate of 5.5% which should apply to restaurants, although Sarkozy might be willing to increase the general rate of VAT which is currently at 19.6% as Angela Merkel did for Germany. There will be certainly more to come.

# Anglo Saxons at the gate

**By Sean O'Connor    August 2007**

Modern western societies have many of the same problems, so not surprisingly their legal systems often come round to providing the same solutions. The following examples could show that French law is creeping towards the Anglo Saxon model.

### Default penalties

Can you, in a French contract, agree upon a whopping penalty for default? To be more precise, can the contract say that if you fail to buy the vendor's house, you will have to pay the full amount of the contract price as a punishment - or can you walk away from the deal?

The old answer to this question was 'yes' because Article 1152 of the French Civil Code says: 'where the agreement provides that the person who fails to perform it shall pay a specified sum by way of damages, there cannot be granted to the other party a larger or smaller sum.'

However, the new answer is 'no' as a second paragraph was added to Article 1152 in 1985, as follows: 'nevertheless, the court can, even acting of its own motion, reduce or increase the penalty that had been agreed, if it is obviously excessive or derisory. Any provision to the contrary shall be deemed not to have been written.'

### Giftwrapped

Can a husband make an irrevocable gift to his wife? Can he give her £100,000 or a diamond necklace on the terms that he cannot take it back?

The old answer was 'no' as Article 1096 of the French Civil Code said that any gifts between spouses were always revocable. Thus if the husband got annoyed with his wife, he could demand the necklace back.

However, the new answer, laid down in a second paragraph added to Article 1096 last year, is that a gift between spouses can in normal circumstances be irrevocable. So now the husband cannot have the necklace back, however enraged he gets with his wife.

There are exceptions to this rule. In particular, if the donee attempts to murder the donor, if the donee commits any assaults on the donor, and if the donee attempts to hasten the donor's death by refusing food to him, the gift can still be revoked.

### Inheritance rights

If you die without children, do your parents have a compulsory right to a portion of your estate? The old answer was 'yes', but since 1 January of this year, those rights have been abolished so the answer is now 'no'.

To continue with the same theme: if you die leaving children, do they have compulsory rights to a portion of your estate? The old answer was 'yes', the new one is 'yes, but'. This is because since 1 January of this year, although the children still have compulsory inheritance rights, they can assign them to someone else. While you are still alive they cannot simply renounce their rights, although they can after you have died.

The effect of this particular change in the law can be relevant to modern conditions. Let us imagine you have remarried and have three children by your first wife. Provided you get your children to agree, they can assign their compulsory inheritance rights to your new wife. They do so by signing, in the UK, a power of attorney in favour of a clerk in the French notary's office. The children can refuse to do so, of course. As I said, it is only by degrees that French law is creeping towards Anglo Saxon attitudes.

All these new positions are the same as those that have long since been adopted in English law except, of course, that in France the compulsory reserves (i.e. forced heirship) have not yet been completely abolished. In general terms, such compulsory reserves have long since been abolished in England.

# Not such a leap of faith

By Philippe Piedon-Lavaux    August 2007

Around 70,000 new-build properties are sold each  year in France. Purchasing a property which has yet to be built or is in the process of being built is known as a *vente en etat fatur d'achevement.* Specific rules apply to such a purchase.

During the conveyancing process purchasers will be asked to sign and go through the following stages:

• the signing of an initial contract with plans and descriptive notice (known as the *contrat de reservation)* by which the purchaser reserves a unit in exchange for a deposit; this is merely a booking form and not a real exchange of contract under French law

• the mortgage documentation (if any)

• the signing of the final deed of sale *(acte authentique or acte de vente),* usually signed within one year of the initial contract and drawn up and signed in the presence of the developer's French *notaire.* This deed of sale makes the purchaser the legal owner of the land and any building works already completed. On completion, a further payment is made; its amount varies depending how far the construction works have gone. Any additional building works will be owned by the purchaser as and when they are constructed.

• the stage payments during the construction works

• the delivery of the keys to the owner.

### The reservation contract

A description of the proposed development, the building and equipment characteristics, plans, price and information about the stage payments should be provided with the initial reservation contract. This gives the purchaser an option to buy the 'proposed and intended development' instead of a specific property. Technical, planning and environmental requirements might still change the property description, plans or even the purchase price of the property.

The purchaser will be bound by his option after a seven-day cooling-off period but not bound to purchase the property and should he decide not to proceed at a later stage, when he receives the final notice for signing the title deed *(acte de vente)* he will only lose the deposit. If the purchaser wishes the developer to tailor the property to his requirements, this should be negotiated into the terms of the initial contract.

Prior to completion the *notaire* will give notice to sign on the title deed. Then the purchaser will have a 30-day period to decide whether or not to complete. If completion is delayed the purchase price might change. Should he refuse to proceed after receiving a second formal notice to complete, he will lose his deposit, otherwise the deposit will be on account and part of the final purchase price.

On final completion it will be confirmed that a definitive planning consent, which cannot be challenged, has been delivered.

Occupation can take place several weeks or months after completion as the property itself will not be finished. The reservation contract has to contain a timescale for the delivery of the property and any specific date.

On completion at the *notaire's* office, the developer will transfer over the rights of the property to the purchaser who will become the owner of the property in its state of progress if works aren't finished yet. The transfer of responsibility will only take place on the delivery of the property.

### Get out clauses

The purchaser is entitled to refuse to complete the purchase and recover the deposit within three months without any additional penalties if:

• the final purchase price is more than 10% than the provisional purchase price

• the vendor is responsible for the sale not completing within the time limits set out in the initial contract

• the loan to fund the purchase is not available or is 10% less than anticipated

• there was an absence of equipment stipulated in the initial contract

• the property is worth 10% less than anticipated (e.g. owing to the quality of materials used or its final layout).

If the developer becomes insolvent prior to final delivery, the guarantor (usually a bank) would complete the works or the developer would fund most of the works before getting paid. Failing that you could withdraw from the contract. This must be confirmed on final completion.

Upon final delivery, the purchaser attends the premises and signs an acceptance form *(proces-verbal de* livraison). If there are any works still to be completed or defects or discrepancies between the contract and the actual completed property, the purchaser should qualify his acceptance by noting this in writing on the acceptance form. The purchasers' rights differ depending on whether the problems result from discrepancies between the description of the property in the contract and the actual finished product (known as *defauts de conformite)* or defects in workmanship.

The law provides for a first class 10-year building insurance in addition to the 10-year professional insurances in place. This will operate regardless of any wrongdoing. Any structural damage will be enough to ensure that the insurance company will pay for the repairs without having to prove that someone did something wrong.

# Index

# Trial 3 issues FREE

*French Property News* is the most widely read magazine for French property hunters, providing **essential reading** and **1000s of properties** for sale every month.

If you are looking for a property in France **look no further!**

Request your **3 issues FREE** trial online – no obligation to buy, but if you like what you read you can subscribe to receive every issue or buy *French Property News* from WHSmith.

## Start your FREE trial today

## www.subscription.co.uk/fpnsample/flaw

# specialist
## french department

The largest team of French lawyers in the UK can help you with:

- buying and selling French property and checking contracts
- off plan and new build properties
- French tax advice
- advice on structure of ownership
- French/UK Wills and inheritance
- settlement of French estates
- divorce and property matters
- French leases

**London**
Watchmaker Court, 33 St John's Lane, London EC1M 4DB

**Portsmouth**
Harbour Court, North Harbour, Portsmouth, Hampshire PO6 4ST

**T:** 020 7814 6932      **F:** 020 7421 1633      **E:** frenchteam@bllaw.co.uk

Also offices in Oxford, Fareham and Southampton

www.bllaw.co.uk

the natural choice in law          Blake Lapthorn Tarlo Lyons